Jesus Ch:

a misnomer of

Lord Krishna of India

(Jesus Story Revisited)

by

Dr. Ravi Prakash Arya

INDIAN FOUNDATION FOR VEDIC SCIENCE
H.O.1051, Sector-1, Rohtak, Haryana, India Ph. 01262-292580
Delhi Contact Ph. Nos.: 09313033917; 09650183260
**Emails: vedicscience@rediffmail.com;
vedicscience@hotmail.com
Website : www.vedascience.com**

First Edition

Kali era: 5014 (c. 2013)
Kalpa era: 1,97,29,49,114
Brahma era: 15,50,21,97,9,49,114

ISBN No.   81-87710-60-8

© Author

Contents

Introduction

While I was preparing the press copy of the English version titled as '*Jesus The Christ was a Hindu*' of the original Marathi book '*Khristache Hindutva*' written by G.D. Savarkar in 1942, I was also attracted towards the character of Jesus the Christ. Based upon the findings of G.D. Savarkar, I carried my researches further in the direction of solving the Jesus riddle. I went through maximum number of books and websites, I could avail on Jesus. They all have been listed in the Bibliography attached at the end of this book. While going through the entire gamut of material available with me, I received conflicting and contradictory views about the person of Jesus. Most of the scholarly findings were relating the legends associated with Jesus the Christ with Lord Krishna of India, others were finding Buddhist element in his teachings and character. Yet another type of studies was negating the historicity of Jesus the Christ. In view of all these conflicting and contradicting findings one gets confused and face a volley of questions as to whether there was no Jesus. If there was no Jesus, how come the events of crucifixion and resurrection took place? Did he really come to India? Was he born to a virgin or not? Was he born on 25th December or some other date? Did he really start preaching at the age of 30? Was he reincarnated from Baptist John? Was he a good shepherd or good cowherd? Whether he was born in Bethlehem or Nazareth? And so on. The present author has tried to answer all these questions keeping in view of the plethora of views woven around Jesus. The present thesis is an improvement upon the G.D. Savarkar's thesis. Savarkar wrote in 1940s. Since then lot of water has flown into Ganges and there was an ardent need to review the Indian-ness of

Jesus the Christ in the light of recent findings which not only doubt the existence of Jesus in the first century CE (Christian Era), but out rightly negate his historicity in the first century CE.

Meantime I also came across a lecture delivered by Bertrand Russell 'Why I am not a Christian' questioning the historicity of Christ. The entire speech has already been placed nest to this introductory note as a prologue to this book for valued readers. Thus, in case of non-existence of Jesus the Christ in first century CE, the Christ centric concept of time calculation becomes irrelevant, so the present author has obliged to convert the Christ Era into Christian Era. In the present book, the dates have been given in the name of Christian Era (CE) and Before Christian Era (BCE).

When the entire gamut of studies is taken into consideration, one will be forced to split the character of Jesus into three parts. There is one Jesus of faith, another is the Jesus of fiction and third one is the Jesus of History.

Jesus of faith has his foundation in the heart of innocent fellow Christians who do not know anything except that Christ is their master only as a matter of faith.

Jesus of fiction lies in the stories propagated by Apostles, Evangelists and Christian Missionaries who want to make a good market out of Jesus.

Jesus of history is standing beyond all fictions and faiths far away from the followers and propagators.

Hereunder, we shall discuss various aspects of Jesus the Christ and try to answer various aspects of his life in the light of new facts coming to

Why I am not a Christian

by

Bertrand Russell

[Russell delivered this lecture on March 6, 1927 to the National Secular Society, South London Branch, at Battersea Town Hall. Published in pamphlet form in that same year, the essay subsequently achieved new fame with Paul Edwards' edition of Russell's book, Why I Am Not a Christian and Other Essays ... (1957). This lecture was first made available by Bruce MacLeod on his "Watchful Eye Russell Page." It was newly corrected (from Edwards, NY 1957) in July 1996 by John R. Lenz for the Bertrand Russell Society which is now available at their page: <http://www.users.drew.edu/~jlenz/brtexts.html>]

As your Chairman has told you, the subject about which I am going to speak to you tonight is "Why I Am Not a Christian." Perhaps it would be as well, first of all, to try to make out what one means by the word Christian. It is used these days in a very loose sense by a great many people. Some people mean no more by it than a person who attempts to live a good life. In that sense I suppose there would be Christians in all sects and creeds; but I do not think that that is the proper sense of the word, if only because it would imply that all the people who are not Christians -- all the Buddhists, Confucians, Mohammedans, and so on -- are not trying to live a good life. I do not mean by a Christian any person who tries to live decently according to his lights. I think that you must have a certain amount of definite belief before you have a right to call yourself a Christian. The word does not have quite such a full-blooded meaning now as it had in the times of St. Augustine and St. Thomas Aquinas. In those days, if a man said that he was a Christian it was known what he meant. You accepted a whole collection of creeds which were set out with great precision, and every single syllable of those creeds you believed with the whole strength of your convictions.

What is a Christian?

Now-a-days it is not quite that. We have to be a little more vague in our meaning of Christianity. I think, however, that there are two different items which are quite essential to anybody calling himself a Christian. The first is one of a dogmatic nature -- namely, that you must believe in God and immortality. If you do not believe in those two things, I do not think that you can properly call yourself a Christian. Then, further than that, as the name implies, you must have some kind of belief about Christ. The Mohammedans, for instance, also believe in God and in immortality, and yet they would not call themselves Christians. I think you must have at the very lowest the belief that Christ was, if not divine, at least the best and wisest of men. If you are not going to believe that much about Christ, I do not think you have any right to call yourself a Christian. Of course, there is another sense, which you find in Whitaker's Almanac and in geography books, where the population of the world is said to be divided into Christians, Mohammedans, Buddhists, fetish worshipers, and so on; and in that sense we are all Christians. The geography books count us all in, but that is a purely geographical sense, which I suppose we can ignore. Therefore I take it that when I tell you why I am not a Christian I have to tell you two different things: first, why I do not believe in God and in immortality; and, secondly, why I do not think that Christ was the best and wisest of men, although I grant him a very high degree of moral goodness.

But for the successful efforts of unbelievers in the past, I could not take so elastic a definition of Christianity as that. As I said before, in olden days it had a much more full-blooded sense. For instance, it included the belief in hell. Belief in eternal hell-fire was an essential item of Christian belief until pretty recent times. In this country, as you know, it ceased to be an essential item because of a decision of the Privy Council, and from that decision the Archbishop of Canterbury and the Archbishop of York dissented; but in this country our religion is settled by Act of Parliament, and therefore the Privy Council was able to override their Graces and hell was no longer necessary to a Christian. Consequently, I shall not insist that a Christian must believe in hell.

The Existence of God

To come to this question of the existence of God: it is a large and serious question, and if I were to attempt to deal with it in any adequate manner I should have to keep you here until Kingdom Come, so that you will have to excuse me if I deal with it in a somewhat summary fashion. You know, of course, that the Catholic Church has laid it down as a dogma that the existence of God can be proved by the unaided reason. That is a somewhat curious dogma, but it is one of their dogmas. They had to introduce it because at one time the freethinkers adopted the habit of saying that there were such and such arguments which mere reason might urge against the existence of God, but of course they knew as a matter of faith that God did exist. The arguments and the reasons were set out at great length, and the Catholic Church felt that they must stop it. Therefore they laid it down that the existence of God can be proved by the unaided reason and they had to set up what they considered were arguments to prove it. There are, of course, a number of them, but I shall take only a few.

The First-cause Argument

Perhaps the simplest and easiest to understand is the argument of the First Cause. (It is maintained that everything we see in this world has a cause, and as you go back in the chain of causes further and further you must come to a First Cause, and to that First Cause you give the name of God. That argument, I suppose, does not carry very much weight nowadays, because, in the first place, cause is not quite what it used to be. The philosophers and the men of science have got going on cause, and it has not anything like the vitality it used to have; but, apart from that, you can see that the argument that there must be a First Cause is one that cannot have any validity. I may say that when I was a young man and was debating these questions very seriously in my mind, I for a long time accepted the argument of the First Cause, until one day, at the age of eighteen, I read John Stuart Mill's Autobiography, and I there found this sentence: "My father taught me that the question 'Who made me?' cannot be answered, since it immediately suggests the further question "Who made god?" That very simple sentence showed me, as I still think, the fallacy in the argument of the First Cause. If everything must have a cause, then God must have a cause. If there can be anything without a cause, it may just as well be the world as God, so that there cannot be any validity in that argument. It is exactly of the same nature as the (Pauranika) Hindu's view, that the world rested upon an elephant and the elephant rested upon a tortoise; and when they said, "How about the tortoise?" the Indian said, "Suppose we change the subject." The argument is really no better than that. There is no reason why the world could not have come into being without a cause; nor, on the other hand, is there any reason why it should not have always existed. There is no reason to suppose that the world had a beginning at all. The idea that things must have a beginning is really due to the poverty of our imagination. Therefore, perhaps, I need not waste any more time upon the argument about the First Cause.

The Natural-law Argument

Then there is a very common argument from natural law. That was a favourite argument all through the eighteenth century, especially under the influence of Sir Isaac Newton and his cosmogony. People observed the planets going around the sun according to the law of gravitation, and they thought that God had given a behest to these planets to move in that particular fashion, and that was why they did so. That was, of course, a convenient and simple explanation that saved them the trouble of looking any further for explanations of the law of gravitation. Now-a-days, we explain the law of gravitation in a somewhat complicated fashion that Einstein has introduced. I do not propose to give you a lecture on the law of gravitation, as interpreted by Einstein, because that again would take some time; at any rate, you no longer have the sort of natural law that you had in the Newtonian system, where, for some reason that nobody could understand, nature behaved in a uniform fashion. We now find that a great many things we thought were natural laws are really human conventions. You know that even in the remotest depths of stellar space there are still three feet to a yard. That is, no doubt, a very remarkable fact, but you would hardly call it a law of nature. And a great many things that have been regarded as laws of nature are of that kind. On the other hand, where you can get down to any knowledge of what atoms actually do, you will find they are much less subject to law than people thought, and that the laws at which you arrive are statistical averages of just the sort that would emerge from chance. There is, as we all know, a law that if you throw dice you will get double sixes only about once in thirty-six times, and we do not regard that as evidence that the fall of the dice is regulated by design; on the contrary, if the double sixes came every time we should think that there was design. The laws of nature are of that sort as regards a great many of them. They are statistical averages such as would emerge from the laws of chance; and that makes this whole business of natural law much less impressive than it formerly was. Quite apart from that, which represents the momentary state of science that may change tomorrow, the whole idea that natural laws imply a lawgiver is due to a confusion between natural and human laws. Human laws are behests commanding you to behave a certain way, in which you may choose to behave, or you may choose not to behave; but natural laws are a description of how things do in fact behave, and being a mere description of what they in fact do, you cannot argue that there must be somebody who told them to do that, because even supposing that there were, you are then faced with the question "Why did God issue just those natural laws and no others?" If you say that he did it simply from his own good pleasure, and without any reason, you then find that there is something which is not subject to law, and so your train of natural law is interrupted. If you say, as more orthodox theologians do, that in all the laws which God issues he had a reason for giving those laws rather than others -- the reason, of course, being to create the best universe, although you would never think it to look at it -- if there were a reason for the laws which God gave, then God himself was subject to law, and therefore you do not get any advantage by introducing God as an intermediary. You really have a law outside and anterior to the divine edicts, and God does not serve your purpose, because he is not the ultimate lawgiver. In short, this whole argument about natural law no longer has anything like the strength that it used to have. I am travelling on in time in my review of the arguments. The arguments that are used for the existence of God change their character as time goes on. They were at first hard intellectual arguments embodying certain quite definite fallacies. As we come to modern times they become less respectable intellectually and more and more affected by a kind of moralizing vagueness.

The Argument from Design

The next step in the process brings us to the argument from design. You all know the argument from design: everything in the world is made just so that we can manage to live in the world, and if the world was ever so little different, we could not manage to live in it. That is the argument from design. It sometimes takes a rather curious form; for instance, it is argued that rabbits have white tails in order to be easy to shoot. I do not know how rabbits would view that application. It is an easy argument to parody. You all know Voltaire's remark, that obviously the nose was designed to be such as to fit spectacles. That sort of parody has turned out to be not nearly so wide of the mark as it might have seemed in the eighteenth century, because since the time of Darwin we understand much better why living creatures are adapted to their environment. It is not that their environment was made to be suitable to them but that they grew to be suitable to it, and that is the basis of adaptation. There is no evidence of design about it.

When you come to look into this argument from design, it is a most astonishing thing that people can believe that this world, with all the things that are in it, with all its defects, should be the best that omnipotence and omniscience have been able to produce in millions of years. I really cannot believe it. Do you think that, if you were granted omnipotence and omniscience and millions of years in which to perfect your world, you could produce nothing better than the Ku Klux Klan or the Fascists? Moreover, if you accept the ordinary laws of science, you have to suppose that human life and life in general on this planet will die out in due course: it is a stage in the decay of the solar system; at a certain stage of decay you get the sort of conditions of temperature and so forth which are suitable to protoplasm, and there is life for a short time in the life of the whole solar system. You see in the moon the sort of thing to which the earth is tending -- something dead, cold, and lifeless.

I am told that that sort of view is depressing, and people will sometimes tell you that if they believed that, they would not be able to go on living. Do not believe it; it is all nonsense. Nobody really worries about much about what is going to happen millions of years hence. Even if they think they are worrying much about that, they are really deceiving themselves. They are worried about something much more mundane, or it may merely be a bad digestion; but nobody is really seriously rendered unhappy by the thought of something that is going to happen to this world millions and millions of years hence. Therefore, although it is of course a gloomy view to suppose that life will die out -- at least I suppose we may say so, although sometimes when I contemplate the things that people do with their lives I think it is almost a consolation -- it is not such as to render life miserable. It merely makes you turn your attention to other things.

The Moral Arguments for Deity

Now we reach one stage further in what I shall call the intellectual descent that the Theists have made in their argumentations, and we come to what are called the moral arguments for the existence of God. You all know, of course, that there used to be in the old days three intellectual arguments for the existence of God, all of which were disposed of by Immanuel Kant in the Critique of Pure Reason; but no sooner had he disposed of those arguments than he invented a new one, a moral argument, and that quite convinced him. He was like many people: in intellectual matters he was sceptical, but in moral matters he believed implicitly in the maxims that he had imbibed at his mother's knee. That illustrates what the psychoanalysts so much emphasize -- the immensely stronger hold upon us that our very early associations have than those of later times.

Kant, as I say, invented a new moral argument for the existence of God, and that in varying forms was extremely popular during the nineteenth century. It has all sorts of forms. One form is to say there would be no right or wrong unless God existed. I am not for the moment concerned with whether there is a difference between right and wrong, or whether there is not: that is another question. The point I am concerned with is that, if you are quite sure there is a difference between right and wrong, then you are in this situation: Is that difference due to God's fiat or is it not? If it is due to God's fiat, then for God himself there is no difference between right and wrong, and it is no longer a significant statement to say that God is good. If you are going to say, as theologians do, that God is good, you must then say that right and wrong have some meaning which is independent of God's fiat, because God's fiats are good and not bad independently of the mere fact that he made them. If you are going to say that, you will then have to say that it is not only through God that right and wrong came into being, but that they are in their essence logically anterior to God. You could, of course, if you liked, say that there was a superior deity who gave orders to the God that made this world, or could take up the line that some of the Gnostics took up -- a line which I often thought was a very plausible one -- that as a matter of fact this world that we know was made by the devil at a moment when God was not looking. There is a good deal to be said for that, and I am not concerned to refute it.

The Argument for Remedying of Injustice

Then there is another very curious form of moral argument, which is this: they say that the existence of God is required in order to bring justice into the world. In the part of this universe that we know there is great injustice, and often the good suffer, and often the wicked prosper, and one hardly knows which of those is the more annoying; but if you are going to have justice in the universe as a whole you have to suppose a future life to redress the balance of life here on earth. So they say that there must be a God, and there must be Heaven and Hell in order that in the long run there may be justice. That is a very curious argument. If you looked at the matter from a scientific point of view, you would say, "After all, I only know this world. I do not know about the rest of the universe, but so far as one can argue at all on probabilities one would say that probably this world is a fair sample, and if there is injustice here the odds are that there is injustice elsewhere also." Supposing you got a crate of oranges that you opened, and you found all the top layer of oranges bad, you would not argue, "The underneath ones must be good, so as to redress the balance." You would say, "Probably the whole lot is a bad consignment"; and that is really what a scientific person would argue about the universe. He would say, "Here we find in this world a great deal of injustice, and so far as that goes that is a reason for supposing that justice does not rule in the world; and therefore so far as it goes it affords a moral argument against deity and not in favour of one." Of course I know that the sort of intellectual arguments that I have been talking to you about are not what really moves people. What really moves people to believe in God is not any intellectual argument at all. Most people believe in God because they have been taught from early infancy to do it, and that is the main reason.

Then I think that the next most powerful reason is the wish for safety, a sort of feeling that there is a big brother who will look after you. That plays a very profound part in influencing people's desire for a belief in God.

The Character of Christ

I now want to say a few words upon a topic which I often think is not quite sufficiently dealt with by Rationalists, and that is the question whether Christ was the best and the wisest of men. It is generally taken for granted that we should all agree that that was so. I do not myself. I think that there are a good many points upon which I agree with Christ a great deal more than the professing Christians do. I do not know that I could go with him all the way, but I could go with him much further than most professing Christians can. You will remember that he said, "Resist not evil: but whosoever shall smite thee on thy right cheek, turn to him the other also." That is not a new precept or a new principle. It was used by Lao-tse and Buddha some 500 or 600 years before Christ, but it is not a principle which as a matter of fact Christians accept. I have no doubt that the present prime minister [Stanley Baldwin], for instance, is a most sincere Christian, but I should not advise any of you to go and smite him on one cheek. I think you might find that he thought this text was intended in a figurative sense.

Then there is another point which I consider excellent. You will remember that Christ said, "Judge not lest ye be judged." That principle I do not think you would find was popular in the law courts of Christian countries. I have known in my time quite a number of judges who were very earnest Christians, and none of them felt that they were acting contrary to Christian principles in what they did. Then Christ says, "Give to him that asketh of thee, and from him that would borrow of thee turn not thou away." That is a very good principle. Your Chairman has reminded you that we are not here to talk politics, but I cannot help observing that the last general election was fought on the question of how desirable it was to turn away from him that would borrow of thee, so that one must assume that the Liberals and Conservatives of this country are composed of people who do not agree with the teaching of Christ, because they certainly did very emphatically turn away on that occasion.

Then there is one other maxim of Christ which I think has a great deal in it, but I do not find that it is very popular among some of our Christian friends. He says, "If thou wilt be perfect, go and sell that which thou hast, and give to the poor." That is a very excellent maxim, but, as I say, it is not much practised. All these, I think, are good maxims, although they are a little difficult to live up to. I do not profess to live up to them myself; but then, after all, it is not quite the same thing as for a Christian.

Defects in Christ's Teaching

Having granted the excellence of these maxims, I come to certain points in which I do not believe that one can grant either the superlative wisdom or the superlative goodness of Christ as depicted in the Gospels; and here I may say that one is not concerned with the historical question. **Historically it is quite doubtful whether Christ ever existed at all, and if He did we do not know anything about him, so that I am not concerned with the historical question, which is a very difficult one.** I am concerned with Christ as he appears in the Gospels, taking the Gospel narrative as it stands, and there one does find some things that do not seem to be very wise. For one thing, he certainly thought that his second coming would occur in clouds of glory before the death of all the people who were living at that time. There are a great many texts that prove that. He says, for instance, "Ye shall not have gone over the cities of Israel till the Son of Man be come." Then he says, "There are some standing here which shall not taste death till the Son of Man comes into his kingdom"; and there are a lot of places where it is quite clear that he believed that his second coming would happen during the lifetime of many then living. That was the belief of his earlier followers, and it was the basis of a good deal of his moral teaching. When he said, "Take no thought for the morrow," and things of that sort, it was very largely because he thought that the second coming was going to be very soon, and that all ordinary mundane affairs did not count. I have, as a matter of fact, known some Christians who did believe that the second coming was imminent. I knew a parson who frightened his congregation terribly by telling them that the second coming was very imminent indeed, but they were much consoled when they found that he was planting trees in his garden. The early Christians did really believe it, and they did abstain from such things as planting trees in their gardens, because they did accept from Christ the belief that the second coming was imminent. In that respect, clearly he was not so wise as some other people have been, and he was certainly not superlatively wise.

The Moral Problem

Then you come to moral questions. There is one very serious defect to my mind in Christ's moral character, and that is that He believed in hell. I do not myself feel that any person who is really profoundly humane can believe in everlasting punishment. Christ certainly as depicted in the Gospels did believe in everlasting punishment, and one does find repeatedly a vindictive fury against those people who would not listen to His preaching -- an attitude which is not uncommon with preachers, but which does somewhat detract from superlative excellence. You do not, for instance find that attitude in Socrates. You find him quite bland and urbane toward the people who would not listen to him; and it is, to my mind, far more worthy of a sage to take that line than to take the line of indignation. You probably all remember the sorts of things that Socrates was saying when he was dying, and the sort of things that he generally did say to people who did not agree with him.

You will find that in the Gospels Christ said, "Ye serpents, ye generation of vipers, how can ye escape the damnation of Hell." That was said to people who did not like his preaching. It is not really to my mind quite the best tone, and there are a great many of these things about Hell. There is, of course, the familiar text about the sin against the

Holy Ghost: "Whosoever speaketh against the Holy Ghost it shall not be forgiven him neither in this World nor in the world to come." That text has caused an unspeakable amount of misery in the world, for all sorts of people have imagined that they have committed the sin against the Holy Ghost, and thought that it would not be forgiven them either in this world or in the world to come. I really do not think that a person with a proper degree of kindliness in his nature would have put fears and terrors of that sort into the world.

Then Christ says, "The Son of Man shall send forth his angels, and they shall gather out of his kingdom all things that offend, and them which do iniquity, and shall cast them into a furnace of fire; there shall be wailing and gnashing of teeth"; and he goes on about the wailing and gnashing of teeth. It comes in one verse after another, and it is quite manifest to the reader that there is a certain pleasure in contemplating wailing and gnashing of teeth, or else it would not occur so often. Then you all, of course, remember about the sheep and the goats; how at the second coming He is going to divide the sheep from the goats, and he is going to say to the goats, "Depart from me, ye cursed, into everlasting fire." He continues, "And these shall go away into everlasting fire." Then he says again, "If thy hand offend thee, cut it off; it is better for thee to enter into life maimed, than having two hands to go into Hell, into the fire that never shall be quenched; where the worm dieth not and the fire is not quenched." He repeats that again and again also. I must say that I think all this doctrine, that hell-fire is a punishment for sin, is a doctrine of cruelty. It is a doctrine that put cruelty into the world and gave the world generations of cruel torture; and the Christ of the Gospels, if you could take him as his chroniclers represent him, would certainly have to be considered partly responsible for that.

There are other things of less importance. There is the instance of the Gadarene swine, where it certainly was not very kind to the pigs to put the devils into them and make them rush down the hill into the sea. You must remember that he was omnipotent, and he could have made the devils simply go away; but he chose to send them into the pigs. Then there is the curious story of the fig tree, which always rather puzzled me. You remember what happened about the fig tree. "He was hungry; and seeing a fig tree afar off having leaves, he came if haply he might find anything thereon; and when he came to it he found nothing but leaves, for the time of figs was not yet. And Jesus answered and said unto it: 'No man eat fruit of thee hereafter for ever' . . . and Peter . . . saith unto him: 'Master, behold the fig tree which thou cursedst is withered away.'" This is a very curious story, because it was not the right time of year for figs, and you really could not blame the tree. I cannot myself feel that either in the matter of wisdom or in the matter of virtue Christ stands quite as high as some other people known to history. I think I should put Buddha and Socrates above him in those respects.

The Emotional Factor

As I said before, I do not think that the real reason why people accept religion has anything to do with argumentation. They accept religion on emotional grounds. One is often told that it is a very wrong thing to attack religion, because religion makes men virtuous. So I am told; I have not noticed it. You know, of course, the parody of that argument in Samuel Butler's book, Erewhon Revisited. You will remember that in Erewhon there is a certain Higgs who arrives in a remote country, and after spending some time there he escapes from that country in a balloon. Twenty years later he comes back to that country and finds a new religion in which he is worshiped under the name of the "Sun Child," and it is said that he ascended into heaven. He finds that the Feast of the Ascension is about to be celebrated, and he hears Professors Hanky and Panky say to each other that they never set eyes on the man Higgs, and they hope they never will; but they are the high priests of the religion of the Sun Child. He is very indignant, and he comes up to them, and he says, "I am going to expose all this humbug and tell the people of Erewhon that it was only I, the man Higgs, and I went up in a balloon." He was told, "You must not do that, because all the morals of this country are bound round this myth, and if they once know that you did not ascend into Heaven they will all become wicked"; and so he is persuaded of that and he goes quietly away.

That is the idea -- that we should all be wicked if we did not hold to the Christian religion. It seems to me that the people who have held to it have been for the most part extremely wicked. You find this curious fact, that the more intense has been the religion of any period and the more profound has been the dogmatic belief, the greater has been the cruelty and the worse has been the state of affairs. In the so-called ages of faith, when men really did believe the Christian religion in all its completeness, there was the Inquisition, with all its tortures; there were millions of unfortunate women burned as witches; and there was every kind of cruelty practiced upon all sorts of people in the name of religion.

You find as you look around the world that every single bit of progress in humane feeling, every improvement in the criminal law, every step toward the diminution of war, every step toward better treatment of the colored races, or every mitigation of slavery, every moral progress that there has been in the world, has been consistently opposed by the organized churches of the world. **I say quite deliberately that the Christian religion, as organized in its churches, has been and still is the principal enemy of moral progress in the world.**

How the Churches Have Retarded Progress

You may think that I am going too far when I say that that is still so. I do not think that I am. Take one fact. You will bear with me if I mention it. It is not a pleasant fact, but the churches compel one to mention facts that are not pleasant. Supposing that in this world that we live in today an inexperienced girl is married to a syphilitic man; in that case the Catholic Church says, "This is an indissoluble sacrament. You must endure celibacy or stay together. And if you stay together, you must not use birth control to prevent the birth of syphilitic children." Nobody whose natural sympathies have not been warped by dogma, or whose moral nature was not absolutely dead to all sense of suffering, could maintain that it is right and proper that that state of things should continue.

That is only an example. There are a great many ways in which, at the present moment, the church, by its insistence upon what it chooses to call morality, inflicts upon all sorts of people undeserved and unnecessary suffering. And of course, as we know, it is in its major part an opponent still of progress and improvement in all the ways that diminish suffering in the world, because it has chosen to label as morality a certain narrow set of rules of conduct which have nothing to do with human happiness; and when you say that this or that ought to be done because it would make for human happiness, they think that has nothing to do with the matter at all. "What has human happiness to do with morals? The object of morals is not to make people happy."

Fear, the Foundation of Religion

Religion is based, I think, primarily and mainly upon fear. It is partly the terror of the unknown and partly, as I have said, the wish to feel that you have a kind of elder brother who will stand by you in all your troubles and disputes. Fear is the basis of the whole thing -- fear of the mysterious, fear of defeat, fear of death. Fear is the parent of cruelty, and therefore it is no wonder if cruelty and religion have gone hand in hand. It is because fear is at the basis of those two things. In this world we can now begin a little to understand things, and a little to master them by help of science, which has forced its way step by step against the Christian religion, against the churches, and against the opposition of all the old precepts. Science can help us to get over this craven fear in which mankind has lived for so many generations. Science can teach us, and I think our own hearts can teach us, no longer to look around for imaginary supports, no longer to invent allies in the sky, but rather to look to our own efforts here below to make this world a better place to live in, instead of the sort of place that the churches in all these centuries have made it.

What We Must Do

We want to stand upon our own feet and look fair and square at the world -- its good facts, it's bad facts, it's beauties, and its ugliness; see the world as it is and be not afraid of it. Conquer the world by intelligence and not merely by being slavishly subdued by the terror that comes from it. The whole conception of God is a conception derived from the ancient Oriental despotisms. It is a conception quite unworthy of free men. When you hear people in church debasing themselves and saying that they are miserable sinners, and all the rest of it, it seems contemptible and not worthy of self-respecting human beings. We ought to stand up and look the world frankly in the face. We ought to make the best we can of the world, and if it is not so good as we wish, after all it will still be better than what these others have made of it in all these ages. A good world needs knowledge, kindliness, and courage; it does not need a regretful hankering after the past or a fettering of the free intelligence by the words uttered long ago by ignorant men. It needs a fearless outlook and a free intelligence. It needs hope for the future, not looking back all the time toward a past that is dead, which we trust will be far surpassed by the future that our intelligence can create.

1
Jesus of Faith

Faith is blind and doesn't want to institute any enquiry about the factual position. Blind faith is not different from superstition. Faith is always subjected to exploitation by its agents. Moreover, it is the blind faith that allows the fabrication of all sorts of fictions. Had there been no blind follower in the world no fiction would have gained ground. Fictions are fabricated when there is market for them. This is a general view. It should not be taken only in case of Christian faith. In fact, faith is fertile ground for fictions. Faith is the prerogative of innocents whereas the fiction is the prerogative of shrewd. In other words, faith is a commodity for marketing and fiction is a technique of marketing to attract more and more consumers of faith. This is why, a big business named as religion is thriving upon various faiths in the world. The more crowd you attract the more business you make. These religions have become only the source of destruction and enmity. We know that there is a temple in every corner of the world and there is crime in every corner of the world. More the religions are becoming strong, more the terrorism is spreading. Faith of innocent people is exploited for the selfish motives and thus innocents are instigated to do all sort of vices in the society in the name of religion. Now a new drama is being enacted by these so called religious heads and that has been named as inter-faith dialogue. Interfaith dialogue means 'An effort to reach some compromising stage by all religious workers so that they may exploit their flocks without being harmed by each other and without coming on the way of each other. The faith germinates in the environment of non-awareness. So the need is to make the people in the world more and more aware about the factual and actual   figures and findings.

Faith, in fact, is a biggest social cancer and its cure lies in awareness and awakening. That is why, a Rigvedic seer proclaims : *vayam raashtre jagriyaama purohitaah.* 'Let us be the awakened leaders in the nation.' But the so called scientifically advanced society of the modern world has been totally blinded by competition of commercialisation not only of science and technology but of everything including faiths and the values, which can also be purchased by money. No one wants to go by the factor of awareness, but everybody weighs everything by money and faith. What to say of human-beings, now there are countries which determine their nationality on the factor of faith.

So long as the factor of awareness doesn't prevail and is not promoted, the Jesus of faith will continue to knock the doors of innocents as strengthened by its agents. In 1954, President Eisenhower harangued his people in the United States to have "faith in faith". When asked to define the faith, all he could manage was a silly statement, " Our Govt. makes no sense unless it is based on a deeply-felt religious faith - and I don't care what it is." (Paul Johnson,1978: 497). Jesus of faith doesn't require any search for his historicity. If such an attempt is made, it is going to be futile one. To quote Michael Amhein (1984:2-3), "By the early twentieth century the so-called 'quest for the historical Jesus' was bogged down in negativism. The Gospels, according to an influential schools of Protestant theologians, were to be taken as theological rather than as historical documents, and they could yield no authentic information about the life and deeds or even the sayings and teachings, of Jesus." The same author further quotes Knox and Nineham, two leading British theologians, who similarly reject the possibility of basing Christian faith upon historical evidence but resort instead to the Church as the basis of faith.

2
Jesus of Fiction

Jesus of fiction was the outcome of the efforts to make the Jesus of faith appear like historical. But there is lot of difference between the term historic and historical. Martin Kahler wrote a book in 1892 titled as "The So-called Historical Jesus and the Historic Biblical Christ". He also made a sharp distinction between 'historical' and 'historic' and poured contempt on the former term. "As far as the Kahler is concerned", comments James P. Mackey (1979:43-44), "It is the business of the Biblical documents to present us with a portrait of the historic Christ. The adjective 'historic', as distinct from its near-verbal neighbour 'historical', indicates not any particular data about the actual man in his time, but rather the impact he has had on the history of the world...Kahler insists that these documents are faith documents, portraying and soliciting faith, that they were never meant to yield historical data about an individual, and that they can never do so in any worthwhile quantity. The tables are turned, but apparently only with the effect of defiantly establishing a thesis which was beginning to be dimly perceived, the thesis that history and faith can find no common ground in research in the origins of Christianity.'

To concretise their faith the rationalists, liberals and modern theologians tried to build up the historical foundation of Christianity. But in the words of Albert Schweitzer (1910 & 1945:2), "The historical foundation of Christianity as built up by rationalistic, by liberal, and by modern theology no longer exists." Thus the historical foundation built by rationalists and others having no longer historic record gave rise to the Jesus of fiction in the artificial history concocted by its agents. But the fictitious history and fictitious facts can live no longer. Moreover the people cannot be fooled all the times. The wider the acceptance that a belief enjoys, the more seeker of truth it has. The truth has to be revealed for its get going. For want of truth it will crumble down like the building with a week foundation. That is why, now the people want to know the truth and for want of truth, "Any one who cares to look", observes Koenaard Elst (1993:1), "can see that Christianity (in the West) is in a steep decline. This is especially the case in Europe, where church attendance levels in many countries have fallen below 10% or even 5%. In most Christian countries, the trend is the same, even if less dramatic. Even more ominous for the survival of Christianity is the decline in the priestly vocation. Many parishes that used to have two or three parish priests now have none. So that Sunday service has to be conducted by a visiting priest, who has an ever fuller agenda as his colleagues keep on dying, retiring or abandoning priesthood without being replaced. The average age of Catholic priests in the world is now 55. In the Netherlands it is even 62, and increasing. This is only partly due to the strenuous obligation of celibacy, for in Protestant churches where priests do get married, and in those countries where Catholic priests ignore the celibacy rules, the decline in priestly vocation is also in evidence. The fact is that modern people just aren't very interested anymore in practising Christianity."

Keeping in view of the above crisis, the custodian of Christian faith are eyeing the east to increase the number of their flock. That is why, church has planned to convert 9 crore Hindus in India into Christianity by the end of 2009. Pope exposed his mind during his visit to India in Oct. 1999 of converting Asia into Christianity in the third millennium. These type of statements only projects the embarrassment faced by church in the west. "In an ironical reversal of roles", reports Arthur J. Pais, "Priests from India are going out to the West, not so much to spread the faith as priests from the West journeyed to the East to do, but to keep the Church's institutions going." He finds, "5000 foreign priests who come on a five year contract negotiated between bishops in America and their respective countries". Among them 500 are from India. "Another 250 (Indian) priests are either working for their master's degree or a Ph.D and work part time in churches, hospitals, schools, prisons and rehabilitation centres, offering religious instructions and counselling. Several of them work as chaplains in the America Armed forces." (Goel 2001: 81).

The same crisis in 1980 was reported after a statistical survey (Barret,1982:7). "Christianity", it says, "has experienced massive losses in the Western and Communist world over the last 60 years. In Europe and North America, defections from Christianity - converts to other religions or irreligion - are now running at 18,20,500 former Christians a year. This loss is much higher if we consider only church numbers : 22,24,800 a year (6,000 a day). It is even higher if we are speaking only of church attendees : every some 27,65,100 church attendees in Europe and North America cease to be practising Christians within the 12 month period, an average loss of 7,600 every day.

At the global level these losses from Christianity ... outweigh the gains in the third world." Here it may also be added in the words of Sita Ram Goel (2001:81) that a large number of churches all over Europe and North America stand abandoned or uncared for. Many churches have been made into buildings for non-religious use. Many others have been sold to non-Christians who have converted them into their own places of worship. The author of present lines has himself witnessed this hard truth in course of his visits to North America. When the American Government did not allow non-Christians to purchase the lands for construction of their respective religious places, the non-Christians purchased the abandoned churches and converted them into their religious places. This author is also the eye witness to the fact that where the churches are not attended by the Christians, they are hired by Hindus for performing their religious prayers and rites. Do you know why this sorry state of affairs is? Or say why has it happened? The point simply is that the credibility of the Church is lost. The awakened people of the West cannot be fooled by factitious stories, since an awakened mind asks for historical evidences and the custodians of Christian faith are no longer able to influence the awakened mind of the West with their fictions. Fictions are fictions. They cannot escape the ravages of time. Faith keeps changing with the change of facts and cannot be tolerated all the times.

3
Jesus of History

Jesus of history stands beyond the Jesus of faith and the Jesus of fiction. The Jesus of faith and the Jesus of fiction cannot have historical roots. So far the agents of Jesus have been trying to convert faith and fiction into history. Recent research negates the existence of a Jesus of faith and fiction. It has been proved that a person named Jesus never lived on earth. Jesus of faith has been a myth. On the other hand there is a discovery in 1887 of Russian historian and itinerant scholar Nicolai Notovich based upon the records and evidences available in Tibet and in India which speaks about the Indian origin of Christianity. Notovich (1895) come across such accounts in the Buddhist texts as describe a person named Issa who came all the way from Israel to India in the company of merchants to learn the lessons on Indian philosophy and Vedas. He took lessons on Buddhism, Jainism and finally learnt Vedas in Jagannath Puri. He visited Rajgriha, Benaras and other holy places during his six years stint of India. The same person became the precursor of Christianity in the West. In the light of all such findings and recent researches, there is a need to revisit the phenomenon called Jesus the Christ. One thing is certain: Jesus as such is a reality, be it mythical, historical, mytho-historical, concocted or superimposed. The author's main aim is to get to the roots of Jesus the Christ (whether of faith or fiction) and the origin of Christianity.

3.1 Jesus' Presence in the Beginning of Christian Era

New researches now prove that both history and tradition are either silent or inconclusive about Jesus' existence. Neither Suctonius, nor Tacitus, nor any of the contemporary Latin or Greek historians, allude to the presence of Jesus or his supposed extraordinary adventures, and yet it cannot be denied that there must have been some strong motivation that guided the pen of contemporary writers.

We may quote here a brief summary of the recent findings that disprove any physical presence of Krisht or Christ in the beginning of the Christian Era (CE).

Many philosophers and scholars have concluded that there was no man named as Jesus who walked on the earth in the first century CE.

It was a group of French philosophers during the   French Revolution in the late 18th century who first concluded that Jesus was a mythical character. Bruno Bauer, a mid-19th century German theologian concluded in part of his four (4) volume set *"Critique of the Gospels and History of Their Origin,"* that Jesus did not exist.

English theologian John M. Robertson, who wrote two books in the very early 20th century, also came to the same conclusion. More recent books on this topic date from 1957 to 1991 and were written by some half a dozen authors. G.A. Wells, a former professor of German at the University of London was one of the more prominent ones. He wrote a series of five books on this topic, arguing that Paul and other First century Christian leaders believed that Jesus had lived in their distant past, perhaps in the 2nd or 3rd century Before Christian Era (BCE). This conclusion/assumption of Paul and other religious leaders of Christianity point to a distant past existence of Krisht/Christ in the 2nd or 3rd century BCE (Before Christian Era). But this author says otherwise. It was not, in fact, the 2nd or 3rd century BCE as claimed by Paul et al but 3000 BCE when Krisht /Christ really walked on the earth in the name of the great Krishna of *Mahaabhaarata*.

The most recent finding that we come across is by Michael Martin (1991). He is a professor of philosophy from Boston University who examined the major beliefs of Christianity. He concluded that there was insufficient evidence to conclude that Jesus existed. Earl Doherty (1999), writing in the Humanist, a Canadian magazine, believes that early Christian leaders saw Jesus as the son of God who was a spiritual being, not a human being. He writes: "If Jesus was a 'social reformer' whose teachings began the Christian movement, as today's liberal scholars now style him, how can such a Jesus be utterly lacking in all the New Testament epistles, while only a cosmic Christ is to be found?" If Doherty's assessment is true, then Christianity would have many points of similarity with other contemporary religions in the world.

3.2 Possible indicators of Jesus' Existence or Non- Existence in the Early 1st century CE

Possible indicators of Jesus's existence or non-existence in the early 1st century CE are as follows:

The Gospel of Q : This is believed by many theologians to be a collection of sayings, "which included moral teachings, prophetic admonitions and controversy stories, plus a few miracles and anecdotes."These had been transmitted orally and are generally believed to have been first written down by his followers in 50 CE. Unfortunately, the Gospel does not include any dates for Jesus' life. If Jesus had been executed in 30 CE, then many who saw and heard him preach would still have been alive and could have verified that the Gospel was accurate. But a case can be made that the Gospel was assembled out of sayings from the 1st or 2nd century BCE.

3.3. Epistles from the Christian Scriptures (New Testament)

Liberal theologians believe that some of these were written as late as 150 CE (up to four generations after Jesus' death) by authors who were not eye witnesses of his ministry. Those writers could have based their findings on traditional sayings attributed to Jesus which were dated from an earlier era. In G.A. Wells' analysis (1986), he was satisfied that the authors definitely believed in the existence of Jesus, but did not cite any evidence that he lived in the First century. They were vague about the location, timing and nature of his birth. Paul does not describe Jesus as a miracle worker, healer or teacher.

Timothy does blame Pilate and "the Jews" for his death. It thus ties the execution of Jesus to a person known to be alive in the First century CE. However, this epistle was written long after Paul's death, and may have picked up the concept from the synoptic gospels which had been widely circulated by that time. Conservative Christians believe that all the books that state they were written by Paul were actually authored by him prior to his death in the mid 60's CE, although there is no evidence that he was an eye witness to Jesus' ministry.

The Canonical Gospels: Liberal and mainline

theologians generally believe that Mark wrote the first Gospel, and that it was composed about 70 CE. Matthew and Luke were authored up to 15 years later. John was written after Luke. None of the authors' identities are known. If these dates are correct, then it is unlikely that any of the authors were eyewitnesses to Jesus' ministry. In spite of their claims, they were relying on secondary sources and accumulated church tradition. Conservative theologians date the gospels much earlier. The Scofield Bible asserts that Matthew was written by a tax collector by that name who was mentioned in Matthew (10:13). Dr. Scofield accepted what he referred to as the traditional date of 37 CE. If the authorship and date are correct, then the gospel represents convincing support that the author was a disciple of Jesus and an eyewitness to his 1st century CE ministry.

The Christian Scriptures (New Testament): Many liberal theologians view the Christian Scriptures as containing some accurate material said and done by Jesus, mixed in with many descriptions of Jesus' sayings and acts that never happened. The latter came from a variety of sources: Religious propaganda directed at enemies of the author's religious group (Anti-Judaic passages in John which imply that "The Jews" are responsible for Jesus' execution is one example); events that never happened, but were added to satisfy prophecy from the Hebrew Scriptures (Old Testament); and the identification of Bethlehem as the birth place of Jesus are some examples).

Other acts and sayings were either distorted versions of Jesus life, or were created from imagination. These were added to bolster the traditions that had arisen within the author's faith group. (Jesus instructing his apostles to baptise in the name of the Trinity is one example.) Material copied from other religions in the Mediterranean area in order to make Jesus' claim to be the God-man. (e.g. the virgin birth, resurrection, status of Jesus as saviour are some examples). Stories of miracles that never happened but were added to bolster the importance of Jesus: for example, raising the dead, or healing people of leprosy, blindness, haemorrhaging, indwelling demonic spirits, etc. Some liberal theologians might believe that there is little or no accurate information about Jesus that has survived into the present. As Bertrand Russell (1927) once said while delivering a lecture on the topic "Why I am not a Christian." on March 6, 1927 to the National Secular Society, South London Branch, at Battersea Town Hall said, "Historically, it is quite doubtful whether Christ ever existed at all, and if he did we do not know anything about him."

The early Christian movement was composed of Gnostics, Jewish Christians, and Pauline Christians. They maintained that God could never take human form. Some denied Jesus' existence as a historical person.

Flavius Josephus: He was a Jewish historian who was born in 37 CE. In his book, '*Antiquities of the Jews*', he described Jesus as a wise man who was crucified by Pilate. Most historians believe that the paragraph in which he describes Jesus is partly or completely a forgery that was inserted into the text by an unknown Christian. The passage "appears out of context, thereby breaking the flow of the narrative." Josh McDowell, Don Stewart and other conservative Christians accept the passage as legitimate. There exists no consensus on a second passage in "*Antiquities*" which refers to Jesus' brother James, having been tried and stoned to death. Some consider it legitimate; others assess it to be a forgery.

Cornelius Tacitus: He was a Roman historian who lived from 55 to 120 CE and wrote the "*Annals*", in 112 CE. McDowell and Stewart accepted his writings as a strong indicator of Jesus' existence in the early 1st century CE. However, the information could have been derived from Christian material circulating in the early 2nd century.

Suetonius: He was the author of '*The Lives of the Caesars*', 120 CE. He wrote, "Since the Jews constantly made disturbances at the instigation of Chrestus, [Emperor Claudius in 49 CE] expelled them from Rome." This passage is often used to support the historicity of Jesus, assuming that Jesus' title was misspelled. But Chrestus was in fact a common Greek name. It is likely that the reference is to a Jewish agitator by that name in Rome.

Other ancient Roman historians: There were about 40 historians who wrote during the first two centuries. With the exception of the above, none stated that Jesus existed in the 1st century.

Jewish literature: The Talmud states that Jesus lived in the 2nd century BCE. However, this passage itself dates from the early 2nd century CE. The authors were probably basing their writings on a reaction to some of the dozens of Christian Gospels circulated by that time.

Jewish Historians: Philo Judaeus lived as the greatest Jewish-Hellenistic philosopher and historian of the time and lived in the area of Jerusalem during the alleged life of Jesus. He was born in 20 BCE and died 50 CE. He wrote detailed accounts of the Jewish events that occurred in the surrounding area. Yet not once, in all of his volumes of writings, do we read a single account of a Jesus "The Christ;" nor do we find any mention of Jesus in Seneca's (4 BCE - 65 CE) writings, nor in the writings of the historian Pliny the Elder (23-79

CE).

Thus, amazingly, we have not one Jewish, Greek, or Roman writer (even those who lived in the Middle East, much less anywhere else on the earth) who ever mentions Jesus during his supposed life time

Pope Leo X (1513-1521): He is quoted by Barbara Walker (1983:471) as having said, "What profit has not that fable of Christ brought us!" Rev. Taylor, in The Diegesis, Page 35, has a slightly different quote from the same Pope: "It was well known how profitable this fable of Christ has been to us."

The Gospel of John disagrees with events described in Mark, Matthew, and Luke. Moreover the book was in Greek near the end of the 1st century, and according to Bishop Shelby Spong (1991), the book "carried within it a very obvious reference to the death of John Zebedee (John 21:23)."

3.4 Internal Evidence Disprove the Historicity of Krisht/Christ in the beginning of Christian Era

Apart from this, there is some internal evidence that disprove the physical presence of Christ in the beginning of the Christian Era.

The Indian Vaishnavite immigrants to Palestine known as Jews inherited from their Indian tradition the concept of Kalki Avataara. Even today, they are expecting a redeemer impatiently. Had a miraculous personality like Jesus been present, they would have recognised this redeemer whom they expected so impatiently. Can it be seriously thought that the Jews would not have hailed Jesus, if he had really performed before them all the miracles assigned to him by the evangelists? Under the circumstances, the story of Jesus Christ's death on a cross like a vulgar demagogue seeking to excite the people against the established authorities is not credible.

4

Origin of Myths/ Legends Associated with Krisht/Christ

If there was no historical Jesus in the beginning of the Christian Era, as discussed above, then from where did the associated myths and legends come? This question has been answered by the scholars hereunder:

According to some, the stories about a number of Jewish prophets and teachers from that Era were consolidated and attributed to one name: Jesus.

According to others, the myths and legends associated with other religious leaders and founders were collected from Egypt, Persia, India, Rome etc. and were rewritten to refer to a person in first century CE Palestine, who may or may not have existed.

Robert M Price (2000) writes: "In broad outline and in detail, the life of Jesus as portrayed in the gospels corresponds to the world-wide Mythic Hero Archetype in which a divine hero's birth is supernaturally predicted and conceived, the infant hero cscapcs attcmpts to kill him, demonstrates his preconscious wisdom already as a child, receives a divine commission, defeats demons, wins acclaim, is hailed as king, then betrayed, losing popular favour, executed, often on a hilltop, and is vindicated and taken up to heaven." He asserts that there are a number of historical and mythical figures whose life stories contain these elements, including Jesus. But just as we do not regard Hercules as a historical figure, a case can be made that Jesus was also a mythical character.

4.1 The Reality behind the Jesus Myth

Now the question arises, if there was no human being named Jesus the Christ in the beginning of Christian era, what is the reality behind this Jesus myth? Even a myth has an origin. No myth can be created from thin air. There was some centre around which this myth was woven. The reality behind this myth will only be revealed when we view the whole phenomenon from the Indo-centric point of view. Everybody should have no hitch in accepting the fact that the Indians in the hoary past migrated from India and settled in the different parts of the Earth. The history of India tells of the large scale migration of various clans of Kshatriyas and Braahmanas, Vaishyas as well as Shudras that took place sometime before the *Mahaabhaarata* war as they searched for new settlements or were ousted from Indian society. The migration from all the four classes of those who were favoured the Kaurvas and also took place after *Mahaabhaarata* war. After the defeat of Kuarvas in the war their supporters left India for the fear of being executed by the winning Pandavas. These clans migrated from India and settled over different parts of the world. The migrating Indians took along with them the various prevailing traditions in cultural, religious, philosophical and social spheres of India of those days. During the *Mahaabhaarata* period Krishna was the most favoured and honoured great man in the world. Before the birth of Krishna, Rama was the most favoured and honoured great man for the people in the world. Both Rama and Krishna are considered as the incarnation of Vishnu. Here, before I proceed further, I seek to clarify that the greatest contribution of Vedic science to the modern world is the concept of reincarnation. The body of living beings is composed of two important things. One is the material physical body, the other is the spiritual body known as soul. Physical bodies die, but spiritual bodies never die. The Soul changes the body life after life. This change of body in laymen's term is known as death. The phenomenon of soul (spiritual body) assuming various physical bodies according to *Sanskaaras* is called reincarnation. A human being can assume the physical body of human beings as well as animal beings in the next life depending on his/her *Sanskaaras*. So, in the Indian historical tradition it is told that Vishnu took birth in the form of Raama in the 24th *Treta Yugaa* (18 Million years ago) and Krishna by the end of 28th *Dvaapara* (5000 years ago).

It is also important to understand that in the earliest period on the earth only two personalities were well known : One was Shiva and another was Vishnu. These two personalities ruled the earth as well as the hearts of the masses. Since then, the people of India got divided into two classes. One class followed Vishnu and another class followed Shiva in their individual and social lives. Followers of Vishnu were known as Vaishnavites or Vaisnava-s and followers of Shiva were known as Shaivites or Shaivas. Rama and Krishna were the incarnation of Vishnu. Before the birth of Krishna, Ram was the Vaisnava ideal. After the birth of Krishna during the period of *Mahaabhaarata*, Krishna assumed the most favoured position among the Vaishnavas in India, although they had full regards for Rama also. In other words it can be stated that by the time of *Mahaabhaarata*, the Vaishnavas in India got divided into Ramites and Krishnites or one can say that Vaishnavism developed into two cults: one around Rama and another around Krishna.

The Indian Vaishnavas who migrated to Rome, Palestine and Arab countries before *Mahaabhaarata* were the ardent followers of Rama. Rama was known by them as Rama Abba (father) or Abba Rama. Same Abba Rama became Abram and Abraham in Palestine. The Ramayanic stories depicted in Roman museums (Arya: 2005) sheds ample light on the Indians who migrated to the western countries pretty well before *Mahaabhaarata* period when Krishna was not yet born.

The wife of Biblical Abraham (Abba Rama), according to a Biblical story, was taken away by Philistine. This Philistine means Pulastyan.

According to the Raamaayana, Raavana was a Paulastya, a descendant of sage Pulista. The word Philistine is used in the same sense in the Bible. A friend of Abraham, according to the Bible, was 'Aner'. Aner is a corrupt form of 'Vaanara'. This Vaanara was Hanumaana. The Bible is not a book of history, so the whole history could not be reported in it. But whatever is stated in short points to Rama-Raavana demonstrates that the groups of immigrant Indians who migrated either before *Mahaabhaarata* war or after it were mostly constituted of Vaishnavas. Pre-*Mahaabhaarata* immigrants were naturally having Rama as their chief. Post-*Mahaabhaarata* Vaishnavas were the followers of Krishna. Thus the former and latter groups got divided into two separate cults: Rama centred and Krishna centred cult. They also started fighting for supremacy. The old group remained followers of Ram, as Vishnu's incarnation. But the latter group, led by St. Paul and Baptist John, tried to maintain their separate identity with Lord Krishna. The latter group started propagating

Krishna-niti (Christianity) or *dharma* as propagated in Geeta by Shri Krishna. Thus Abraham of old immigrants and Krisht (Christ) of neo-immigrants were historical personalities of the remotest past back home in India. As such Abram and Jesus the Christ cannot be called mythical characters.

Yes, if the historians and researchers tries to find the history of Krisht (Christ) close to the beginning of Christian Era, they would certainly be disappointed and fail to do so. Under the circumstances they will have no alternative save to say that no Krisht (Christ) existed in history. Krisht/Christ was not an earthly human being etc. The history of Krisht/Christ who existed 3000 years Before Christian Era (BCE) cannot be written by historians of the beginning of Christian Era (CE). So Krisht/Christ of the Christian Era is mythical, whereas Christ of 5000 years ago is a reality.

Here it is important to note that from the name 'Jesus the Christ', 'the' was lost and only Jesus Christ became prevalent after a lapse of some period. Jesus Christ means Keshao Krishna.

Thus, Christianity was constructed over the revival of the Krishna cult in the West. This fact may further be elaborated with the following evidence.

That all the stories prevalent about the historical Krishna were also associated with the life of Krisht (Christ) with some changes and twists according to the prevalent social and political requirements by St. Paul and Baptist John and their disciples to show down the rival group of Ramites (Abraham). Some of the examples can be cited hereunder :

1. Prophecy about the birth: There was a prophecy about the birth of Krishna. Similarly the

Krisht /Christ's life was also foretold by the prophets.

2. Killing of children: Kansh, tyrant of Mathura, was fearful that the new-born Krishna would dethrone him some day. He thus commanded the massacre of all male children born on same night as Krishna. Herod, the king of Judea was similarly motivated to kill all the children of two years and under in Bethlehem and around the country. (Matthew Chapter, 2). It may be pointed out here that this version attributed to Herod has been handed to us only by Apostles, i.e. only by those who had an interest in reviving the Krishna cult instead of the Rama cult. Contemporary history has nowhere recorded this audacious crime.

3. Safe escape of the child: Vasudeva and Devaki left Mathura to save the Child, Krishna. Krishna appeared before the Kansh at the age of 12 and killed him. In a similar narrative, Joseph and Mary fled to Egypt to save the child, Jesus, from massacre, and did not return until after the death of Herod. At the age of 12, Christ astonished the doctors in the temple by the wisdom of his answers.

4. Birth: Krishna was born at 12 O' clock night, similarly Krisht /Christ was also born at night (Luke: 2:8).

5. Miracle man: Krishna has been depicted as a miracle man who performed numerous miracles. Similarly Krisht (Christ) was also projected as a miracle man. He changed water into wine at the marriage of Cana, resuscitated Lazarus, three days after the latter's death; the son of the widow of Naim, healed the lame, restored sight to the blind, hearing to deaf, and cast out devils from those possessed.

6. Titles: Krishna had two titles - Keshava and Deva. Still the title of Keshava is more prevalent in Tamilnadu. In the language of Indian immigrants to Arabia and Europe, Keshava corrupts as Jeshav. From Jeshav becomes Joshua then Jeshva, Jeosua, Josias, Josue etc. which finally becomes Jesus. Similarly Deva transforms as Zeus which again goes along with Jesus. In a similar vein, Krisht (Christ) was called Keshava or Jesus.

7. Premonitions of divine birth: The mother of Krishna had a premonition that a great divine personality was taking birth from her womb; similarly the mother of Krisht (Christ) also had a premonition of the divine birth of Krisht.

8. Viraataroopa darshana (Transformation): Krishna revealed his Viraata roopa to Arjuna, who was in a dilemma in the war of *Mahaabhaarata*. Similarly Krisht (Christ) is said to have transformed himself before Peter, James and John on a high mountain. His face was shining like a sun, and his vestments became white as snow.

9. In Shrimad Bhaagavata Puraana, Krishna is said to have been approached by the Gopis to adore him; similarly Krishna of Palestine, i.e. Krisht or Christ, was approached by Jews for the same purpose.

10. Christ's birth-place: Lord Krishna was .born in Mathura. Likewise, the Krishna of *Mahaabhaarata*, Christ was also born in the city of Bethlehem. Bethlehem is nothing else but the corrupt form of Mathura. The word Mathura, while travelling to the west got corrupted into the Bathura and Bathura transmuted into Bathula. Bathula became Bethlehem. Thus Mathura> Bathura> Bathula> Bethlehem.

12. Revival of Indian memories of Krishna in Palestine: Apart from Bethlehem, Jesus is also said to have born in the village of Nazareth. This village is said to be located in a beautiful valley where the river Kissen flows down the slopes of the mountain Tember, in Palestine. There was no village named Nazareth at the time when Krisht/Christ is said to have born. This clearly points out that the above mentioned story is not related to Christ but to Krishna. Krishna was born in Nandigrama that became Nazareth in the memory of the Indian immigrants. Nandigrama is located at the banks of river Krishna or Yamuna. Yamuna is also named as Krishna after the name of Shri Krishna. All over India, the name 'Kissen' is used for 'Krishna'. The river 'Kissen' appears to be a corrupt form of 'Krishna'. The river Krishna in south India also stands for Yamuna recognising Shri Krishna as the pan-India factor of respect, just as Madurai in South India is the revival of the memories of Mathura in North India. Similarly one can say that the village Nandigrama was revived as Nazareth, and the river Krishna was revived as Kissen in Palestine by the then Indian Immigrants.

13. Parentship of God and Devotion

shrinvantu vishve amritasya putraah
ye dhaamaani divyaani tasthuh

The concept in these lines of the *Upanishad* is repeated in the statement of Christ that 'I am the son of God'. He saw God as his father. In the '*Shrimad Bhaagavata*' all sorts of imaginative relations are applied to God according to individual mentality. With those relations the devotees worship God. Devotees imagined God as father, mother, friend, husband, wife, master etc. and worshipped in this mode in order to gain *siddhi*. Similarly, Jesus the Christ was related to God as his son. His mother Mary had faith that her husband was a divine personality. It means she was a wife of the God.

Christ too supposed that his father was God because of firm belief in his mother. Therefore naturally he believed that he was the son of God.

Such, according to evangelists, are the chief events in the life of Jesus the Christ/Keshava the Krisht, which are apparently a second edition of the same facts and acts already attributed to Krishna of ancient India. Marvelling at this close similarity of attributes of Krishna and Krisht (Christ), Louis Jacolliot (1876) had to declare that the Christian Church's borrowing system is but a second edition of the Indian church.

In addition to the above similarities in the life of Krishna and Christ, the apostles of Christianity also borrowed many characteristics of Vaishnavism from back home in India to their Vaishnavism in the west (known as Christianity). Some of the points of similarity are:

1. The Indian concept of the Trinity of God (Brahma, Vishnu and Mahesha) was taken by Indian immigrants to the west and the same was introduced in the ideas of the revived Krishna cult called Christianity.

2. Regarding Christian baptism, Louis Jacolliot (1876: 315) questions, "Is Christian baptism is anything else than Hindu baptism (Dikshaa)?".

3. The adherents of Krishna have the sacred Yamuna river; similarly Christ and his followers have the sacred Jordan river.

4. In India, ancient priests were religious judges, received public confession of faults, and adjudged the penalty. The functions were arrogated by the Apostles. They also established public confessions, as is commonly known, first time in Church. It was not until more than two centuries after the beginning of CE that the bishops substituted private persons for public confessions -

an occult agency whose demoralising tendency is too easily indicated.

5. The Indian priest is anointed with consecrated oil, practises the tonsure, and receives investiture of the sacred thread. The Apostles do the same to distinguish from the lay believers.

6. The Vedic concept of *Sarvamedha* (purification of all) transfigures in a corrupt form in the Vaishnavites of west, as the sacrifice of mass.

7. The revolt of Devas against Brahmaa was registered as revolt of angels in the Vaishnavites of the west (Christians).

8. **Similarities between Bible and Geeta**: It is interesting to note that the Bible (Old Testament) quotes 'Gheeda' for borrowing some philosophy. There, Gheeda means the 'Geeta' and nothing else. The New Testament shows many verses which are similar to Sanskrit verses. For example, 'even a lame can climb a mountain' is a statement in the New Testament, which is similar to a Sanskrit *Subhaashit* (popular saying) *'panguh langhayate girim'* meaning 'a lame can climb a mountain'. If we collect such statements and compare with the *Geeta* or the *Upanishads*, we may find the truth.

9. **Vedic teachings reflected in Krishna cult of west (Christianity):** Vedic Dharma emphasises *ahimsaa* (non-violence), *asteya* (non-stealing), *satya* (truthfulness), and purity of sexual relations (*brahmacharya*), and respect for elders (*vriddha-sevaa*), *kshmaa* (forgiveness). It prefers the righteous to the unrighteous. *asto maa sad gamaya* meaning "Lead me from unrighteous to righteous." It prefers *aparigraha* (non-hoarding of wealth) to hoarding. All these values travelled with Indian immigrants to the west in the teachings of their Krisht/Christ. Their Christ also forbade murder, theft, bearing false witness and illicit sexual relationship. He also insists that elders must be

held in high esteem. He advocates mercy and is against accumulation of futile 'treasures upon earth'.

10. **Krishna speaks through Christ:** Christ of emigrating Indians speaks in the words similar to Krishna of *Mahaabhaarata*. Krishna tells in Geeta, "Those who believe me and love me are certain to reach me after death (means attain moksha). Those who believe me can be sure of salvation." Christ of immigrant Indians make remarkably similar promises as recorded in John's Gospel. "He that heareth my word, and believeth on him that sent me, hath everlasting life, and shall not come into condemnation; but is passed from death unto life' (John, 5:24). And 'He that believeth in me, though he were dead, yet shall he live' (John, 11:25).

11. **Buddhist elements in the Christ of Indian immigrants:** Post-*Mahaabhaarata* Indian immigrants in the west not only endowed their Krishna (Christ) with the Vedic values and character of Krishna of *Mahaabhaarata*, but they also epitomised their Christ with the miracles of Buddha prevalent among the then Mahaayaana Buddhism. Some of them are cited here.

At one place Buddha says to his disciples, 'Those who have ears to hear, let them hear'. They perform miracles: the sick are healed, the blind regain their sight, the deaf hear again, and the crippled walk freely. He steps across the Ganges in flood. Christ of Indian immigrants also walks across the waters of the lake. His disciples also perform miracles, just like their predecessors, the disciples of Buddha.

On one occasion Buddha comes to the bank of a river. From the opposite bank a disciple who had been unable to find a boat begins walking across on the top of water towards him. He begins to sink when his meditative concentration on Buddha was disturbed. He was saved when he managed to regain his absorption in contemplating the Master. The people who witnessed the event were astounded. Buddha said, 'It is faith that leads us across the flood waters, wisdom brings us safe to the other side'. Similarly Peter, a disciple of Christ of Indian immigrants, approaches Christ by walking on the water. Peter also begins to sink when his faith started to waver. He was saved by the supporting words and arms of Christ. The people who witnessed the event were also astounded there. Walking on water is a Yogic concept which is possible after some *saadhanaa* (yogic practice), according to *Yoga Darshana* of Patanjali. This concept is peculiar to India.

There is one particular story about Buddha that represents, according to Holger (1994:100), a most amazing parallel between the older Buddhists texts and the New Testsmant. It is known as the parable of the Widow's Mite. According to the Buddhist version, there is a religious assembly at which the faithful are required to make financial donations. The wealthier members of the congregation give generously and in valuable coin. There is a poor widow, however, whose total possessions amount only to two small coins, and these she duly gives with pleasure. The presiding priest perceives her noble gesture and publicly praises her for making it, saying nothing at all about other donations. The corresponding passage in Mark's Gospel tell it this way:

And Jesus sat over against the treasury, and beheld how the people cast money in the treasury: And many that were rich cast in much.

And there came a certain poor widow, and she threw in two mites, which make a farthing.

And he called unto him his disciples, and saith unto them, verily I say unto you, That this poor widow hath cast more in, than all they which have cast into the treasury:

For all they did cast in of their abundance; but she of her want did cast in all that she had, even all her living.   (Mark, 12:41-44)

The close similarity between the two versions confirms a borrowing from Buddhists sources.

After Buddha's death, theological disputes broke out between Sthaviras and Mahasanghikas. The religious council was convened in Rajagriha. The orthodox Buddhists formalised their doctrine at the council of Pataliputra some 300 years after Buddha's death. In pretty much the same manner, after the declaration of the death of Christ of Indian immigrants, theological disputes broke out between Jewish Christians (Vaishnavite followers of Rama) and Hellenist Christians (Vaishnavite followers of Krishna). They also convened a religious council in Jerusalem. Christian church at the council Nicea was seen in 325CE, that is 300 years after the so called death of Jesus.

The fact is that around the beginning of the Christian Era, Mahaayaana school of Buddhism had just evolved from Hinayana sect of Buddhism. It was Mahaayaana school of Buddhism that turned Buddhism as a universal religion, open to believers of every nation and background. Mahaayaana philosophy focuses on compassion for all beings, as embodied in the ideal of the Bodhisattva, a concept that had taken place in 3rd century BCE. The Bodhisattva is the enlightened one who defers his merging with the universal being, who postpones his Nirvaana so long as it takes for him to lead everyone to the path of salvation. The earthly existence of Boddhisattva has the single purpose of leading all souls on to the path of moksha, the path that constitutes liberation from the cycle of rebirths and sufferings.

The Indian immigrants in the west were also attracted to the growing popularity of Buddhism in the west. They assigned all those qualities that characterise a Bodhisattva to their Krisht/Christ. That is why their Christ also became the epitome of the Bodhisattva ideal.

5

Jesus' Life-Events Revisited

5.1 Tragic End of Jesus

After knowing the reality behind the Jesus myth one would naturally seek an explanation on the various life-events associated with the life of Jesus. For example, if John the Baptist and St. Paul were propagating Krishna cult in the name of Krishna-niti (Policy of Krishna narrated in Geeta) or Christianity, then what was the need to propagate the tragic end of their legendary hero and prove his contemporaneity by falsifying the facts?

It seems that by selling the tragic end of their legendary hero, the Krishna group wanted to gain sympathy from the common man in order to increase their numbers over the Rama Group (Abraham) of believers.

5.2 Crucifixion

The next question that perplexes the minds of readers is that if no human being named Christ existed and if Christ was the revival of Krishna of *Mahaabhaarata* in the west, what was the need to weave the story of crucifixion just to show the tragic end of the Jesus to gain more sympathy for the propagation of their cult? This burning question has been examined by many scholars in the west itself. It has been found after careful examination of the history of social and political traditions in Palestine and other countries in the west that crucifixion was not a new phenomenon peculiar to Jesus, but it was a common rite in the ancient Palestine in which a human being was sacrificed in the name of Jesus (Joshua) son of Keshava, the God (Robertson, J.M. 1966, Introduction by Hector Hawton, p.5). Here it may not be out of context to point out that this tradition in ancient Palestine was carried by Indian immigrants from Vedic concept of Purusha medha which is wrongly translated as human sacrifice in its literal sense. There is a *Purusha Sookta* in the *Rigveda* and *Yajurveda* which explains the process of creation from the *Purusha* (God). In the Vedas *Purusha* means God and not the human being. The process of manifestation of *Purusha* in the form of created world is known as *Purusha medha*. This Vedic concept was carried by the Indian immigrants to west in the form of cosmic sacrifice. In the tradition of Jews the crucifixion symbol was used as the symbol of cosmic sacrifice.

Fig.1 : Picture of cosmic sacrifice used by Jews
Source : Goswami (2000)

Later on this symbolic description of cosmic creation became the capital punishment that rulers used over their subjects.

Josephus, the historian of Jews, had written that Alexander Jannaeus used to crucify Jews. G.A. Wells (1985:198-99) observes, "Jannaeus' crucifixion of eight hundred Pharisees left a particularly strong impression on the Jewish world".

The death on the cross was thought by the Romans to be the most demeaning and frightful form of execution. Cicero called it the most horrible and repulsive kind of punishment. Only in exceptional cases, were Roman citizens ever sentenced to this punishment, and only those from the lowest social strata. But in the lands occupied by Romans, crucifixion was a favoured deterrent, to keep the rebellious people obedient. Palestine had long been notorious as a place of nationalist unrest. From the time of Maccabees in 167 BCE until Bar Kochba in 134 CE, there were some 62 rebellions, wars and uprisings against the pagan yoke; first that of Greeks and then that of the Romans. Sixty one of these disturbances started from Galilee, the (so called) home area of Jesus. (Holger, 1994:243-244)

Moreover in Christianity this symbol was adopted quite late in the 13-14th century of Christian Era (CE). This also shows that crucifixion had nothing to do with the Krishna cult made prevalent in the beginning of CE in the west by the neo Indian immigrant Vaishnavites.

5.3 Was Jesus a Shepherd?

When there was no person in existence named Jesus in the first century CE, and the Jesus in 5000 BCE was not a Shepherd, then how come shepherd-ship was associated with the Krisht/Christ of the Indian immigrants in the west? The answer is that just as various attributes were borrowed from various sources from different countries and assigned to Jesus, similarly he was called a shepherd by the followers of the Buddha. On one occasion, Buddha while preaching to his favourite disciple Ananda, referred to himself as 'a shepherd full of wisdom' who bends down to redirect those of the flock who are wandering towards the abyss(Holger,1994: 96).

Fig. 2 : Bodhisattva as the Good Shepherd.
Source : Holger Kersten (1994)

Due to the attribute of shepherd assigned by Buddha to himself, the (Bodhisattva) has been depicted as a good shepherd in some of the figures found outside India at   Turfan in east Turkestan (today the Chinese province of Sinkiang). See fig. 2 above.

Thus the propagator of Krishna in the west who were from Essene cult and were influenced by Buddhism depicted their Krishna as a good shepherd. They borrowed this attribute of the shepherd from Buddha and assigned it to their Lord.

5.4 Jesus was born to a Virgin on 25ᵗʰ December

Some theologians and historians believe that many of the details of Jesus' life were "borrowed" from a competing, contemporary religion, Mithraism. Mithra was a fictional character who was worshipped as a Good Shepherd, the way, the Truth and the Light, the Redeemer, the Saviour, and the Messiah. A religion in his name was founded in the 6th century BCE. Mithraism was one of the more popular religions in the Roman Empire, particularly among its soldiers and civil servants. It was Christianity's leading rival. Mithra was also believed to have been born of a virgin. His birth day was celebrated yearly on Dec. 25. Similarly, the propagators of the Krishna cult saw their Christ as being born of the Virgin on Dec. 25. Mithra was also visited by shepherds and by Magi. He travelled through the countryside, taught, and performed miracles with his 12 disciples. He cast out devils, returned sight to the blind, healed the lame, etc. Symbols associated with Mithra were a Lion and a Lamb. He held a last supper, was killed and buried in a rock tomb. He rose again after three days, at the time of the spring equinox, March, 21. He later ascended into heaven. Mithraism celebrated the anniversary of his resurrection. The Christian Easter ceremony is the imitation of this Mithiraism. They held services on Sunday. Rituals included a Eucharist and six other sacraments that corresponded to the rituals of the Catholic Church. Scholars believe that the followers of Krishna cult (Christianity) may have appropriated many details of Mithraism in order to make their religion more acceptable to Pagans. St. Augustine even stated that the priests of Mithra worshipped the same God as he did.

6
Christ or Krishna

On the basis of the information thus far presented, one can safely conclude that the story of Christ was nothing more than the revival of Krishna of Mahaabhaarata in the west and Christianity is nothing else but the revival of tenets of Geeta in the west. Many western scholars who have pursued unbiased studies on this disputed matter have reached similar conclusions. According to Louis Jacolliot (1876), the Jesus legends coined by the evangelists do not mention the name Christ right from the beginning of the birth till his death. Only after his death, was Jesus called Christ by his apostles. According to the same author, the name Christ was appropriated by the Apostles after the name of the son of Devakee, i.e. Krishna. The same author further elaborates as under:

'We write Christna rather than Krishtna, because the aspirate 'kh' of the Sanskrit is philologically better rendered by our 'Ch' which is also an aspirate, than by our simple 'k'. In it we are therefore guided by the grammatical rule, and not by the wish to produce a resemblance.

On the question of Christ being derived from the Greek Christos, the above cited author explains as under:

'Besides that most Greek words are pure

Sanskrit, which explains the resemblance, wherefore this choice of a Greek surnom for Jesus who, a Jew by birth, passed his militant life and died in the midst his compatriots? The only logical conclusion is that this name of Christ was a part of the complete system adopted by the Apostles - to construct a new society on the model of primitive Brahminical religion.'

Constantin François de Chasseboeuf, de Volney (1757-1820) a philosopher, historian, and politician was one of the earliest writers to question the historicity of Christ. Hector Hawton in his introduction to a reprint of Pagan Christs by J.M. Robertson (1966:5), points out that Voleny of France concluded in the 18th century that "Jesus was a solar myth derived from Krishna of Hindus." J.M. Robrtson, a British scholar and a Member of Parliament, confirmed Voleny's thesis in 1900 by stating in his "*Christianity and Mythology*" that "the Christ Myth is merely a form of the Krishna-myth". (Schweitzer,1945:290-91fn.)

At one place, Paul blames Jesus' death on Satan and demons, rather than the Roman government. This belief of Paul suggests that he was not referring to a person who lived close to his life time but to the Lord Krishna whose follower he was.

At another place, Paul wrote that he received personal revelations directly from Jesus, presumably in the form of visions. This statement of Paul clearly points out that he is not referring to any person born in his time, but referring to the Lord Krishna born in the remote past.

6.1 Some More Evidences

Krishna was a Kshatriya in whose tradition the sacred thread ceremony is performed at the age of 12 years. Christ's sacred thread ceremony was also performed at his age of twelve years. The ceremony is called Sabath of Phylacteries and was performed in a temple. Jesus is also sketched with a *Yajnopavita* or a sacred thread on his left shoulder hanging downwards. These pictures are seen in the Uffizy Gallery of Florence and are painted by an Adele artist in the tradition of Perugino artist. It is also present in the Ampule of the Cathedral of Mozart.

Fig. 3: Uffizy Gallery of Florence

Fig. 4 : Cathedral of Mozart

As is described in the Gamera of Banilova, Jesus was a 'Sidta' or 'Sidda', i.e. a 'Siddha'. *Siddha* is a famous Sanskrit word used for a spiritually high ranked Yogee, a perfected sanctified man, This is exactly the characteristic of Krishna. Krishna is called as Yogiraaja 'king among yogis'.

'Baala Krishna' is often depicted as holding the sign of Tilak on his forehead. Jesus the Christ depicted in the paintings prepared in the 11th century and included in the Venetian Bible covered with ivory cover and in the paintings prepared in the 13th century, displayed in a Cathedral of Pist. In these paintings Jesus is shown with the Tilak mark on his forehead. This proves that Krisht/Christ was none other than the revival of the Krishna character and Christianity is nothing else but the Krishna religion of immigrant Vaishnavites in the west. Had he not been the handiwork of immigrant Indians, then he would not have been depicted with Tilak marks on his forehead and the European artists would not have painted Tilak on his forehead. Of course he was depiction of Krishna by the immigrant Indians in the west. This is why he was depicted with such marks on his body and so, traditionally, he was painted with the typical Hindu marks on his body like a sacred thread, Tilak on the forehead etc.

Christ is called as 'Good Shepherd'.

Fig. 5 : Good Shepherd, Catacomb 3rd C

Fig. 6: This fresco of the Good Shepherd was found on the ceiling of the Vault of Lucina in the Catacomb of Callixtus in Rome.

Good Shepherd means a man rearing cattle with care in a good manner. Krishna was Gopal i.e. a cowherd. The followers of Krishna cult revived Krishna. Therefore following Krishna's name, Jesus was also called as 'Gopal' which means a cowherd or a shepherd. Gopal includes rearing and protecting cows as well as sheep, goats, buffaloes etc. At the time of his birth, the cowherds and shepherds came to see him. There is more evidence for this. We find at many places the paintings of Jesus prepared by European Christian artists, in which Jesus is sketched as a baby like 'Baala

Krishna'. Christ as a smiling child is portrayed just like smiling Baala Krishna. In a similar fashion one Italian artisan Kentucky Sansovino has carved a sculpture of Christ as a child which is kept in St. Augustine Modanna at Rome. In this sculpture, Jesus is shown with a dark complexion. Since Christ was the revival of Krishna, he was depicted with dark complexion after the fashion of Krishna. In Christian literature, it is said that Christ was of whitish colour. To confirm what is this whitish colour we have to see a portrait displayed in Saint Sylvester Church in Rome where he is shown with a complexion just like Krishna and of course like Tamils from South India.

Fig. 7 : Saint Sylvester Church in Rome

In a book authored by G.D. Savarkar (2003:65), there is some discussion about the title of Christ. The author has shown that the word 'Hannazeri' is a combination of 'Annam+ Asari' = Unna + Assari = Annasari = Hannasari. The word 'Asari' is a corrupt form of 'Acharya'. In Tamil also, Sanskrit word 'Acharya' is corrupted into Assari. Acharya, in

Sanskrit, means elder or teacher. In Pseudo-Matthew's Gospel, in its first part, it is recorded that the grandfather of Christ's mother and the great-grand-father of Christ was titled as 'Achar'. The western scholars are flabbergasted by word, but there should not be any dispute about the fact that 'Achar' is a corruption of the Sanskrit word 'Acharya'. The Sanskrit word 'Acharya' gets transformed in Tamil as 'Assar or Achar'. This title was applicable to Krishna. This is also strong evidence to confirm the hypothesis that Christ was none else but the revival of Krishna of Mahaabhaarata.

7
Actors of Jesus Drama

If Christ were the revival of Krishna and Christianity were the revival of Krishna-nity, then the question arises, who scripted the Jesus drama and why?

As already mentioned in detail in the foregoing pages, St. Paul and John the Baptist were the main choreographers of the Jesus drama. In this drama John acted as Jesus and Paul acted as the propagator. They revived Krishna to dismiss their Ramite brothers (followers of Abram). This fact is strengthened by the following observations.

For Mark's Gospel to work, for instance, you must believe that Isaiah 40:3 (quoted, in a slightly distorted form, in Mark 1:2-3) correctly predicted that a stranger named John would come out of the desert to prepare the way for Jesus. It will then come as something of a surprise to learn in the first chapter of Luke that John is a near relative, well known to Jesus' family. (Bible Review : June 1997 : 43)

The above statement in the form of prophecy clearly shows that John prepared the way for the story of Jesus.

John was a very influential and successful preacher of his times. He had a large following. He started propagating the Krishna religion effectively. When people asked about Krisht or Jesus, he used to say that Krisht/Christ is a messiah in waiting. These statements of John led Herod arresting him in 31CE. Somehow or the other, John escaped from the dungeon of Herod and never made a public appearance as John the Baptist for fear of being executed by Herod. Instead, he disguised/transfigured himself with the name of Jesus as per his public declarations to prove the truth of his prophecy. This fact can be confirmed from the following statements of Gospels of Mark (1.14), Matthew (4.12) and Luke (4.14f) (Holger Kersten and Elmer R. Gruber,1994 : 240). Gospels say that people even occasionally thought he (Jesus) might be the reincarnation of John. Jesus emancipated himself from John after the latter's arrest, when he emerged from the shadow of his teacher and went his own way.

The above statement projects Jesus as the reincarnation of John. It also talks about the emancipation of Jesus from John after his (John's) arrest. Here it may be remembered that the phenomenon of reincarnation or emancipation doesn't take place quickly within days or months. It requires many years passing through the cycle of death, rebirth and attaining the youthful age. These statements only confirm John the Baptist's disguise as Jesus as per his declaration after his escape from Herod's dungeon. John also propagated that he baptised Jesus at the age of 30 in 30CE. In 31CE John was arrested and was said to be executed. Here it should be noted that no incarnated person can attain the age of 30 years after one year of being incarnated. As such Jesus could not have attained the age of 30 years as an incarnation of John the Baptist just one year after John's death. The fact is that John escaped Herod's dungeon and appeared with the name of Issa, a synonym for Jesus.

One more point may also be noted here. John the Baptist never directly called himself Jesus

(Keshava) whose religion he was propagating. He used to introduce himself as Issa in the west and both Issa and John in the east. Since he belonged to the Essene or Ishaana religion of the west, he used to introduce himself as the Issa John. This will be clarified and proved in the ensuing pages.

'Issa' means having affiliations to an Essene or Ishaana religion. So he called Krishna as "Issa Christ" meaning 'Krishna propagated by Essenes'. There is no denying the fact that John the Baptist had his links with the Essenes. Essenes were the Shavites in Palestine. Ishaana is the name of Shiva in India. Those followers of Ishaana were known as Essenes or Issa. In view of the same fact, John the Baptist was also named 'Iso Mhesia' which appears to be a corruption of   'Isha Mahesha' or 'Ishaana'.

One more clue to prove this fact can be had from the *Raajataranginee*, an ancient work on the history of Kashmir by Kalhana. It counts as one of the earliest genuine historical records in the Sanskrit literature of India. The *Raajataranginee* relates the history of a holy man named Ishaana, who performed miracles. He is said to have saved the influential statesman Vazir from death on the cross, and to have brought him back to life. Afterwards, Vazir became the ruler of Kashmir and governed for 47 years. According to Kalhan, Ishaana was the last reformer in Kashmir, and lived and worked in the 1st century CE. This historical narration of *Raajataranginee* unveils the mystery behind the story of Issa's escape from death on the cross and his miracles. It was not the so-called Jesus of the west but some Yogi in Kashmir who did all these miracles and saved a Vazir from death on the cross and not Issa himself who was saved from death on the cross. But due to the similarity of names, some scholars like Holger used this evidence to prove Jesus' presence in Kashmir. This is all confusion and does not confirm the historicity of Christ and his visit to India.

7.1. Some more Evidence to prove that John the Baptist acted as Jesus

According to Pliny the elder and Josephus, the Nazarene sect flourished on the banks of Jordan and on the eastern shore of the Dead Sea for at least 150 years BCE. Its followers were permitted to keep long hair. Perhaps they never cut it all, like many Hindu ascetics (Holger,1994: 82). John the Baptist is depicted with long hair, and wearing 'raiment of camel' hair, and a leather girdle about his loins' (Matthew, 3:4). The description of Jesus given by a Roman patrician named Lentulus in a letter to the Roman senate is similar to that of John the Baptist. In the Epistle of Lentulus, Jesus' hair is described as 'flowing and wavy'; it fell loose over his shoulders, and was 'parted in the middle of head after the fashion of Nazarenes'. The description of Jesus and depiction of John the Baptist confirms the hypothesis that John the Baptist (after 31 CE) had escaped the Herod's imprisonment by disguising himself with the name of Jesus, the messiah in waiting (as he declared himself). Here it may be pointed out that Nazarenes (first propagator of Christianity), who were from Essenes cult, added the Buddhist element to the form of Christianity propagated by them, since Essenes were a Shavite sect of Hindus influenced by Buddhist teachings. That is why Buddhism influenced the Krishna cult (Christianity) propagated by John the Baptist (who was an Essene) and his followers. In view of the same facts, Jewish historian Heinrich Graetz even described Christianity as "Essenism with foreign elements' (Holger,1994: 82)

7.2 Consequences of Drama

This Jesus drama took a dramatic turn when

John the Baptist became popular as the prophesied Jesus. The growing popularity of John in the form of the new messiah could not be tolerated by Paul who was also one of his associate in this drama. The string of the Jesus drama went out of the hands of Paul and was completely captured by John. Paul, who came from a strict Jewish family and had acquired Roman citizenship through his father and paid a high price for it, could not tolerate this forgery by an Essene and he turned foe of John as well as his followers. He called himself and his followers as 'true believers' and John and his followers as 'non-believers', because he followed his mission in right earnest whereas John went astray and projected himself as a messiah. This forgery by John made Paul impatient zealous, fanatic and intolerant. He opened up a deep rift between 'true believers' (himself) and 'non-believers' (John). He became a most vehement opponent of the John whom he saw as an obstacle to his mission. Paul even went so far as to apply to the high priest for special permission to persecute the followers of John beyond the city limits of Jerusalem hoping that the great zeal he intended to display in carrying out this task would also make an impression on the religious hierarchy (Holger Kersten,1994:28). Due to his fanaticism and intolerance against 'non-believers', he was christened as 'epitome of intolerance' by a theologian A. Deissmann (1925).

Here it may also be pointed out that the concept of redemption from sin (which causes suffering in the world) by the vicarious sacrificial death of Jesus in the Christianity was Paul's contribution. According to Holger Kersten (1994 : 232), "It is precisely this form of the doctrine of salvation in traditional Christianity that rests almost exclusively on the work of Paul, and was never taught by Jesus." Holger is correct in pointing out this fact, but he forgets that the introduction of this concept of redemption of sin by vicarious sacrificial death of Jesus by Paul was the part of his plan to prosecute John for committing the sin of impersonating Jesus. In other words, Paul wanted this falsehood to die. That is why, he taught that the whole function of Jesus centres on his sacrificial death, that through the shedding of his blood he has absolved the faithful of their sins and released them from chaos and domination of Satan. (Holger, 1994: 232).

Paul is blamed for placing little emphasis on the actual words and teachings of Jesus (expounded by disguised John) and being too preoccupied with his own teachings. He is also blamed for putting Jesus (disguised John) on a pedestal and creating him into the Christ figure. Unfortunately, his critics failed to unravel the truth behind the whole drama. Paul knew that no Jesus had descended upon earth, but it was John who was misguiding the innocent people. So, he never cared for the teachings of the disguised John. Rather, he continued with his teachings of the Shri Krishna. It should be remembered that the designation of Krisht/Christ to Krishna was given by Paul and the designation of Jesus /Keshava was given by John. Paul's chasing of John and attempting to get him (John) persecuted compelled him (John) to leave the country and return to his dreamland i.e. the original land of his ancestors (India). He followed some caravan and reached India.

Thus the Krishna cult was split into two streams, from its very birth in the west - Pauline Krishna cult or Paulinism and John's Krishna cult. Paulinism called Krishna as Krisht/Christ whereas John called Krishna as Jesus/Keshava. Paulinism remained confined to the West, whereas John shifted to Tibet and India. That is why, critics say that what is called Christianity today is largely the artificial teachings of Paul, and should more correctly be called Paulinism. Wilhelm Nestle (1947:89), the religious historian, makes the point by saying, "Christianity is the religion founded by Paul; it replaced Christ's Gospel with a Gospel about Christ." The first part of Wilhelm Nestlé's observation is true, but the second part shows a lack of facts. Had he been informed rightly, he would have observed that Christianity is the Krishna cult founded by Paul. There is no question of replacement of any Gospel by Paul. Paul was a true man. This confusion was created by John who started propagating Krishna cult by embodying himself as Keshava/Jesus. Paulinism had the shadow of Krishna, whereas John's has the shadow of Buddhism. The Buddhism aspect of Christianity is the contribution of John and the Krishna aspect is the contribution of Paul. Thus Pauline Krishna-niti (Christianity) is certainly different from John's teachings of Krishna, the Keshava/Jesus, although both have their roots in India and are the part of the great philosophical thought of India. Modern Christianity only developed when Paulinism was promulgated as the state religion.

7.3. Difference between Paulinism and Christianity
propagated by John

John was an Essene and Essenes were an Indian Shavite sect. In the Vedic system, the *Dikshaa* rite is very important. A newcomer is always given *dishes*. This initiation rite was also prevalent among Essenes. This rite is performed by sprinkling waters. Essenes called it a baptismal rite. The meaning of *dikshaa* or baptismal rite was to relieve a person from ignorance and sin. *Apastamba Shrauta Sootra* defines *dikshaa* or baptism as : *anritaad satyam upaiti atha dikshitam bhavati.* That is, when a person, relieved of his sins and ignorance, redeems the truth, he is said to be *dikshita* or baptised.

Since John the Baptist belonged to Essenes, the Indian sect, he believed in baptism. That is why, he exhorted the people to repent for their sins and to receive baptism at his hands in waters of the Jordan. For John, baptism was the way out for relief of sins. But for Paul the way out was something else.

According to Paul, nobody can be relieved of his sins until and unless the blood is shed. He was apparently pointing to the punishment of John, who was misguiding the people by posing himself as the Christ (Krishna) in the west. He meant that John could have relieved from his sin (of betraying the innocent people by posing himself as Christ) only through capital punishment on the cross.

8

Nicolai Notovich's
Discovery Needs Review

Towards the end of 1887, the Russian historian and itinerant scholar Nicolai Notovich reached the Himalayan state of Kashmir, in northern India, on one of the many journeys to the orient. He discovered some scriptures about the mysterious prophet Issa in Hemis monastery in Tibet. This book tells in detail how Issa arrives in Sind (the Indus) in the company of merchants, and he settled among the Aryans, in the land of beloved of God, with the intention of perfecting himself and of learning from the laws of Buddha. Issa, according to the book, travels through the land of five rivers (Punjab), stays briefly with the erring Jains, and then proceeds to Jagannath, where the priest honoured him with Joyous reception. At Jagannath, Issa learnt Vedas. But there he invited the displeasure of Braahmans by imparting instructions to Shudras. After spending six years in Jagannath, Rajagriha, Banaras and other holy places, he deserted those Braahmanas who were unhappy with his (Issa's) teachings that God doesn't judge the worth of human beings by their caste but by their ability to do karma. The book further describes how Issa repairs further to the Himalayan region, to Nepal, where he remains for another six years and dedicates himself to the study of Buddhists scriptures. Finally he moves on towards the west, passing through various countries as an itinerant preacher, preceded well in advance by a celebrated reputation. He also stands upto the priests of Persia, who expel him one night with the hope that he will quickly fall a prey to wild animals. But providence allows Issa to reach Palestine safely, where the wise men inquire of him, 'Who are you, and where do you come from?' We have never heard of you and do not know even your name.' 'I am Israelite,' Issa replies. 'I returned to the land where my parents lived, in order to bring my brothers back to the faith of our ancestors, a faith which enjoins us to be patient on earth so that we might achieve the consummate and highest happiness here and hereafter.'

The above description of the books discovered by Notovich in Tibet clearly points out the fact that John's ancestors belonged to India. He came to India to learn the faith of his ancestors and returned to the country of his parents to bring his brothers back to the faith of their ancestors, a faith which enjoins them to be patient on earth so that they might achieve the consummate and highest happiness here and hereafter.

Dr. Notovich took photographs of pages of that book and after returning to his home he printed three copies of each page from the negatives. Thus he prepared three copies of that unique book. That book records reports of Issa in India for seventeen years. It also has included one short book written by Issa himself. One of the copies of this book was sent to the Pope by Dr. Notovich. Pope kept it for six months and then wrote him that he has burnt the book because it should not be published. Dr. Notovich had earlier smelled such mischief so he had prepared three copies. Later he published that book under the title *'The Unknown Life of Jesus'*. But it was banned by the American Government feeling that it may harm the Christian mind. It is better to give one more information here. Arther Lily has authored a book named as *'India is Primitive Christianity'*. He states there,'Christ was an Essenes. Like Indian Yogis these Essenes also tried hard to merge with the Brahman, the supreme Being or to meditate in seclusion to know the Brahman.' Further he adds, 'The Essenes resembled the Gurus, the spiritual masters of Brahmanism'. The above mentioned book of the 'Hemis Monastery' is a copy of a book in Persian language from 'Marboor Math'. In the book of the Hemis Math there are in all two hundred forty four (244) verses and is divided in fourteen chapters. It has reported some information which is given in short here:

> *'When Issa attained the age of thirteen, his parents tried to arrange his marriage. But he wanted to follow celibacy (Brahmacharya). Therefore he left the house at the age of thirteen years. He aimed at salvation like Buddhists or Brahmins. To attain it, he travelled in caravan to India in company of merchants. He stayed for some time with Jain Sadhus. Then he wandered to Jagannath Puri. There he followed the path of celibacy (Brahmacharya) and studied the Vedas. By this time he completed twenty years of his age. Thereafter, he went to holy places like Kashi, Prayaga, Rajagriha, etc. to live with Sadhu-Santas and to visit some more holy places. After this he entered Bauddha Vihar and stayed there for six years to study that cult. Finishing that study he travelled to Nepal, Tibet, etc. He studied there too and then he returned to his birth place. He combined non-violence of Buddhists, philosophy of the Vedas, devotion of lord*

Shiva and Yoga Saadhanaa to lay down a cult. He wanted to spread this cult so he returned to his country."

The story in this book cannot be assigned to Christ, but Baptist John is the actual subject matter of this story. John was a Hindu *Samnyaasee* who might have come to India in his early age as described in the book and he might have adopted Hinduism.

8.1. John the Baptist as an Indian Samnyaasee

Sydney Heath (1907), an author, writes, 'Sometimes our Lord is painted with 'reddish yellow attire' *(Kashaaya-vastra)* like the Vedic Samnyasins'. This colour is the famous and pious orange colour of the Vedic people. In the basilica of Saint Paul Cathedral at Rome, a portrait of Christ is depicted in an orange coloured robe with a stick in his left hand and with a special style of his right fingers bent forwards. (Savarkar, 2003:72). The exact meaning was not deciphered by European scholars that on the bank of the river Jordan, Saint John made himself known as Jesus. This process was described as the initiation of Christ at the hands of John. Saint John was in fact a believer of Hinduism. G. D. Savarkar (2003:72) explains the Indian element in his name. Jnaana which is a Sanskrit word very difficult to speak or write in other languages and scripts. Hence it is pronounced in Hindi and rural Marathi to Gyaana Jnaana is a compound word formed from 'j'+'n'. This is not accurately pronounced anywhere. In Marathi it is pronounced as d+n+y. In other regions also the letter gets corrupted. Even then the compound nature of the letter remained intact in India in one or the other form. However, when the letter travelled to the western countries, the compound nature of the same was lost. 'N' disappeared while 'j' remained intact. Jnaana became Jaana, while Jaana converted into John. Saint means a holy person. It is derived from Sanskrit term 'Santa'. The meaning of the Sanskrit term 'Santa' is transferred to 'Saint'. This evidence may not be accepted by all thinking it to be caused by the slippery of tongue. As such, of more evidences can be given to prove that Saint John was of Indian origin.

1] In the Cemetery of Pontius in Rome there is a painting of sixth century AD in which the hermitage of Saint John is depicted with grazing deer. It is well known that ancient Indian sages, Munis and Samnyasis domesticated deer in their hermitages which had a playful time with them.

2] A picture of about 500 AD is preserved in a Cathedral of Milan wherein Saint John is depicted wearing a Dhoti on his waist and an upper garment just like the Indians.

3] In the museum of Arles, in the third Chapel, there is a landscape painted in fourth century depicting a ceremony of Baptism. In it St. John is seen with a skin (of a tiger or deer) on his body. This is a typical Indian (Vedic) style.

4] A similar scene of Baptism is cited in a picture depicting the initiation of Santa Maria. This is displayed in Novena of Cosmedin. It depicts St. John wearing a spotted skin of a deer or leopard. Thus St. John was depicted as Indian Samnyaasee. He is said to have given *Deekshaa*, initiation to a Christ, on the bank of the river Jordan in 30CE. A scene depicting this consecration is painted in a picture displayed in the basilica of Saint Paul in Rome. In this painting Christ is portrayed with an orange coloured robe on his body, one 'Kamandalu' (an urn) to store water in his hand and an alms-dish or a begging bowl in other hand. This painting is described by F.W Farrar (1874:352). This is clearly a picture of an Indian Samnyaasee. John the Baptist in later stage of his life after 31CE posed himself as Jesus.

8.2 John's Relationship with the Naatha Cult of Bengal

Naatha cult came into existence long before the beginning of Christian Era (CE). It was founded by Matsyendranaatha and Gorakshnaatha. The Naatha cult, particularly the Bengalese in the Naatha cult sing a devotional song (*Bhajana*) traditionally which is as follows :

Aave kona dyaashene eeshei gela?	Which country Issa went?
Phirale kava?	When did he return?
Karane gela jane?	Where went John?
Aave kunathee gela yogeer yogee?	Where went Yogi's Yogi?
Magne tora mana?	Where is your mind?
Aave aarova dyaashe eeshei gela?	To Arabia Issa is gone
Phirale mari	Died but returned
Mishra dyaashe jana	To Egypt went John
Aave eeshei aamaara gurur guru	Issa is our Guru's Guru
Yogeer yoge thaake mana	Let mind be in Yogi'sYoga

The above cited poem describes a person named as Issa with his synonym as John. This proves beyond doubt that the person who visited India in the name of Issa was none else but John the Baptist. John mentioned in the poem is undoubtedly John the Baptist, no explanation is needed for it. According to GD Savarkar (2003:104), in India whatever is presented in a form of poetry never perishes with time. Nothing new can be added to that poetry. It is a speciality of Indian tradition. It is for this reason that the forms of cults did not change or vanish during centuries or millennia. In spite of passage of a vast period the original form of any cult is still preserved in India. If this peculiar fact is borne in mind, we must remember that the person who came to India was not Jesus the Christ, but John the Baptist. Issa was not the nomenclature for Christ, but John the Baptist. The above mentioned Bengali poem clearly names the person as John and his synonym as Issa. This poem clearly proves that John the Baptist, himself being an Essene, had his relations with the Naatha cult in India. Notovich, the author of the book '*The Unknown Life of Jesus Christ*' and Holger Kersten (1994:20) though talks about the Jesus' connection with the Natha cult of India, but they did not go through the poem and fail to quote the poem. The poem was first quoted by G.D. Savarkar (2003:104) in his famous book '*Jesus the Christ was a Hindu*'. The poem clearly shows the connection of John with Naatha cult and not of Christ. The whole thesis of Notovich and Holger Kersten turns upside down. Naatha cult is established primarily by Lord Shankar according to the book namely '*Nava Naatha Bhaktisaara*'. It is also quoted in the tradition or genealogy of Gurus in the Naatha cult that Lord Shankara established this cult. John the Baptist belonged to the Essenes' cult in Palestine. It has already been clarified that Essene cult was a Shavite cult. The very term Essene evolved from the Sanskrit word 'Ishaana', the name of Shiva. When John during his visit to India came to know about the existence of Naatha cult, it was natural that he came close to this Indian counterparts of his cult. He might have visited this cult in view of the similar origin of his

Essenes' cult. The line of Gurus is remembered every day by the Yogis in Naatha cult. In the incarnations of Lord Vishnu, Krishna is given the prime place and Krishna is supposed to be the complete incarnation of Vishnu.

According to G.D. Savarkar (2003:105), in the Vindhya mountain at difficult places there reside some Yogis of the Natha cult. They have a book in their possession titled as *'Naatha Naamaavalee'*. Some portion of it was seen by a famous Sadhu of Bengal Shri Vijaya Krishna Goswamiji who was contemporary to Shri Ramakrishna Paramhansa. In a magazine *'Pravaasee'* in its issue of Maagha lunar month Bengali *Shaka* 1333, an article titled as 'Seventy Years' was published. In this article some information is given relating to the above mentioned book *'Naatha Naamaavali'*. The same is quoted here :

'Issa came to India at the age of fourteen years and studied for sixteen years when he was given a 'Darshan' by Lord Shankar. Thereafter he went back to his country and preached greatness of God. But while doing this great work, the ignorant people did not heed to him. On the contrary, they tried to prosecute him. Ishanaatha's trouble was sensed by a great Naatha Yogi 'Chetan Nath' in his Samaadhi in India. He travelled the distance of three months in only three days with his yogic power and appeared in Israel. When Chetan Nath appeared in Israel, there were earth-quakes and other portentous phenomena boding calamity. In that critical condition Chetan Naath took Isha Naatha out of dungeon, and escorted him safely to India.

This information was propagated by John during his stay in India. Accordingly, he came to India at the age of 13, studied here and returned to his country, but was prosecuted there. The same information became prevalent in the Indian and Tibetan records which is being quoted as proofs. The above information was published by Swami Abhedananda.

8.3. Who died in Kashmir?

Baptist John came to Kashmir. He met Chetan Nath, a Yogi of Naatha cult and with his help he established one Math (Monastery) at the feet of the Himalayas probably in Kashmir. He worshipped Lord Shhiva there for three years. He gathered knowledge and energy and placed Trishhoola, a seed of the world. He worshipped Lord Shhiva in the form of a Linga. Sadhus and people came from all directions to stay with him and accepted him as Guru, the spiritual teacher. This way he carried the work of the cult till he died. The Bhajan of Naatha cult calls him as John and Issa. *Naatha-Naamaavali* quotes his name as Ishanaatha.

This proves the Indian credentials and root of John proving him a Hindu beyond doubt.

8.4. Jesus of Nazareth ?

In most translations of the Bible, Paul is shown hearing a voice on the road to Damascus that says, "I am Jesus of Nazareth, whom thou prosecutes". (Holger,1994:79). From this statement one thing is quite clear that the Jesus of Nazareth who was prosecuted was different from Jesus of Bethlehem, around whom the whole story of Krishna cult of west (Christianity) revolves. The above statement shows the intention to relate Jesus to his place of origin. As such he should have been described as Jesus of Bethlehem. Moreover it may also be pointed out here again that there was no place known as Nazareth during first century CE in Palestine nor do we find any evidence in support that Jesus ever lived in Nazareth. On the other hand Greek manuscripts mention a Jesus titled as

Nazarene. So now the question arises as to who was this Jesus of Nazareth mentioned in Greek manuscripts as Jesus Nazarene. The researches have also established (*Greek-German Dictionary of the Writings of New Testament and other Early Christian Literature*, 1963) that there is no possibility of finding any linguistic connection between the expressions Nazarene and Nazareth. So there is a difference between Nazareth and Nazarene. Holger Kersten (1994) tries to assimilate both the terms in the name of Jesus of Bethlehem. The term of Nazarene has been explained in the Acts of Apostles.

In the Acts of Apostles, the first Christians are called Nazarenes (Holger,1994:79). Through this evidence it is also clear that first Christians were called as Nazarenes. Jesus the father of Christianity cannot be called as first Christian. Only the persons who first of all started propagating the tenets of Christianity can be called as Nazarenes. As such St. Paul and John the Baptist and others can be included in the category of Nazarenes. Here it is interesting to note that John the Baptist was known as a prophet to Nazarenes, and was also known as the 'saviour' in Galilee. Flavious Josephus (XVIII, 5:2) describes the Baptist as

" ... *an honourable man, who inspired the Jews to do good and to treat each other well, and who urged them to receive baptism. Then, he declared, God would look with favour on the baptised - for baptism conferred physical healing and was not merely the washing away of sin. Atonement for sin must come beforehand, and must centre on the leading of a virtuous life. Massive crowds thronged around John, much moved by what he said...."*

Thus from the above evidence it can unhesitatingly be stated that Jesus the Nazarene was John the Baptist. John, as pointed above, was known as saviour in Galilee. As such the statement of Mark's (6:1) Gospel - that Jesus's followers lived by the sea of Galilee, probably in Capernaum, for it is of thereabouts that it is said and he .... came into his own country - only talks about John the Baptist who was the saviour in Galilee.

8.5. Who were Essenes?

Since John the Baptist who played the role of Jesus was an Indian and belonged to a Shaiva cult in the west known as Essene, so it is necessary to know about Essenes and their philosophy.

The people of this cult were known as 'Tera-puet'. This word means the eldest. It is corruption of a Sanskrit word '*Sthavira Putra*', or '*Thera Putta*' of Paali language. In the past the name was used for a branch of Buddhists in Europe. Buddhism was a cult, a branch of the Hindu religion, just like Shaivism, Vaishnavism, etc. and not a separate religion, different from or in contrast with the Hindu religion. Therefore it seems that both Buddhists and Shavites were merged with Essene cult. There were many experts in Yoga, Ayurveda, Botany etc. and their branches, which were useful for the people in general. To help people in agony they used their knowledge of medicine, Ayurveda, botany etc. They loved seclusion and peace. Only to help people or to give them knowledge they used to contact them, otherwise abstained from meeting public. They lived in mountains, caves, forests, secluded places etc. For maintenance they depended on agriculture or gardening. They had ideal virtues, properties and were devoted to the truth and honesty. They avoided trickery or cheating, they had spiritual knowledge, and had no desire except to help people. According to honesty and virtues, they were divided in four ranks. Many of them observed celibacy, though some were married. For entering the cult, hard tests had to be given. A new-comer had to undergo rigorous hardships to prove his natural good character. It was expected that a person following their rules should not be in trouble; but the moral rules should become their nature. Their routine practice was to get up early at dawn from bed, wash mouth and face, go to toilet, take bath, and pray God. After prayers they put on clothes proper to their business. At mid-day they returned home, washed their hands and feet, and wearing clean white clothes they took lunch. Their earnings and business were common. In a way, they were socialists, but their socialism was not physical, crude and hypocritical.

It was a spiritual, moral, ethical, philosophical comradeship. They strictly observed their rules and regulations, according to ranks. If anybody departed from the rules and behaved wrongly, he was expunged from the rank of the cult. Their ranks were graded according to the spiritual position and capability. When they met, each saluted saying, 'Let peace be with you' (*Shaantirastu*). That prayer for peace was for all. They said, 'Let peace and prosperity be with you'. This appears to be translation of Sanskrit saying '*Shaantirastu, 'Pushtirastu'*. It was the rule that the highest ranked man must be at the top of spirituality. It was supposed to be the fourth rank. This fourth rank controlled all the members of the lower three ranks. The experts of the fourth rank selected the best person among them, supposed him to be head and worked under his authority. Members of the lower three ranks led their life virtuously, following celibacy, truth, charity, much away from selfishness and troubling others. They craved for morality, merits and good qualities, for which they practised religious austerities. As they rose to higher and higher position in spirituality, they attained upper and upper rank, till they entered the fourth rank possessing ideal character and the highest moral altitude. All these members of Essene cult and particularly the fourth rank sages were calm, quiet, happy, genuinely honest, loving, kind, merciful, decent, polite. They were respectful and merciful. They were ornamented with wisdom, divine virtues, and knowledge of various sciences. The Essenes were adorned with excellence, divine qualities, very useful for the society, helping all community, donating everything to people. Therefore they became very popular. However they remained aloof and quiet on the spiritual path. They had a definite aim for their life and were capable to achieve it. They were ready ever to sacrifice their life for the altruistic cause. They had no fear at all. Selfishness, deceit and degradation were great sins for them. To quarrel among themselves or with others and vengeance were unknown to them. John was a member of this cult. He was a Samnyaasin, a distinguished personality. In that cult, the first and second rank included many people, children and aged ones, rich and poor, merchants, industrialists, farmers, servants, etc. but all were good natured. The cult flourished in Egypt, Palestine and countries around, in which there were many monasteries and seminaries along with colonies of Essene people.

8.5.1. Fourth Rank Essenes

In India the real great Yogis are rarely seen, similarly in Palestine and countries nearby the Essenes of the fourth rank were not easily seen. Rarely on some occasion they used to appear before a particular person. In his presence or in a dialogue with him a man felt that he is experiencing something divine. The fourth ranked Essene used to wear a white robe. They used to appear unexpectedly, used to remain in contact with a selected man for a limited necessary time, used to go away immediately after finishing work, into seclusion, and it was done in a calm and quiet manner without having any desire or expectation in mind. Therefore it was natural that people thought them to be divine, superhuman. Any ordinary common man held them to be angels or Good men. Those high ranked Essene Yogis always loved seclusion, so they lived in impassable region in forest or mountain or in caves. Here it may also be mentioned that this forth rank was nothing else, but the *Tureeyaavasthaa* as called in the Indian system of yoga. A Yogee of *Tureeyaavasthaa* was termed as Essenes of fourth rank by the immigrant Indians in Europe.

9

Review of Muslim Sources

Savarkar (2004: 144-147) quotes an Arabian book titled as 'Tarikh-i-Azami' which states, 'There is a famous lake on the boundaries of Kashmir and Afghanistan, called as 'Ishanalaya' 'house of Shiva'. There every year in Caitra lunar month, at the time of Sun's entry in the sign of zodiac 'Aries' i.e. *Mesha Sankraanti* day, assembles a big crowd for worshipping Lord Shhiva. While touring to India, Issa was thirsty and he quenched his thirst by drinking water of this lake. He became fresh again. The crowd gathers here in memory of that incident.' This description of the Arabian book establishes relationship of John the Baptist (Issa) with the Shiva cult which was prevalent in west as Essene cult.

At the time of Mohammed Paigambar's birth around five to six hundred CE, only Vedic religion was prevalent in Arabia, though it was in its corrupt form. We find much information recorded about Issa as a passing remark in Koran. In Koran at verse 645, a famous Moulana Mohammed Ali states in foot notes thus: This verse states that Jesus did not die on cross. He remained alive. Even then assuming him to be dead, his body was handed over to his friends. In the same Koran, verse 1723, in the notes, it is stated with evidence that messiah finally came to India in Kashmir and died in Kashmir. The evidence is recorded as follows :

(A)   At a high altitude from the sea level, there is a fertile land having many ponds and lakes. Christ went to such a country. The description points to lands like Jerusalem, Egypt, Damascus, etc. But those were not the countries where Christ went. It was Kashmir where Christ resided.

(B)   Ten human species are now lost from Palestine.   Some of them are found in Kashmir. Some names of villages and towns of Palestine are given after the fashion of names of the villages and towns of Kashmir. Therefore it is not unnatural that Jesus from Palestine came to India in Kashmir. In Srinagar, there is a street called as 'Khanayar', where there is a Samaadhi, a tomb, which is named as tomb of 'Nabi saheb', or Paigambar or Issa or Yus-Asaf Nabi. Muslims believe that no Paigambar came after Mohammed. Paigambar from any other country or religion did not come in Kashmir, any time. Issa was the closest Paigambar born before Mohammed. Therefore the tomb of NBA must be the tomb of John called as Issa. Moreover it is also called as tomb of Issa. As already observed that Issa do not mean Christ but John the Baptist. But since now the whole story has become prevalent in the name of Jesus which is contribution of John himself, everybody takes it granted for Christ. Nobody knows about John who posed himself as Jesus during the visit to his ancestral land (Bharat).

Now why is it called as tomb of Yus-Asaf ? The reasons given by Moulana Mohammed Ali are as follows :

(a)   A traditional legend in Kashmir tells about the presence of a Paigambar named as Yus-Asaf two thousand years ago. The tradition also relates the tomb to that of Yus-Asaf.

(b)   The Arabian book known as *'Tarikh-i-Azmi'* (p.82) records the tomb to be of one Paigambar who was a king named as Yus-Asaf.'

(c)   Another Arabic book titled as *'Ikmaba Udadin'* is about a thousand years old. It states that Yus-Asaf went to a distant country.

(d)   Relying on an ancient evidence Joseph Jacobus states that Yus-Asaf (Isaseph) finally went to Kashmir and expired there.

(e)   *'Barlaam and Josaphat'* (1913:9) shows that the tomb on the main street, named Khanayar, is of Yus-Asaf. But who was this Yus-Asaf? Asking this question, Mohammed Ali states, 'The written and oral evidence shows that he was a Nabi or Paigambar, beyond suspicion. There is marked resemblance between 'Yus' and 'Yeshu'. Yeshu is an Arabic conversion of Jesus. The philosophy of Yus-Asaf and Jesus are miraculously similar. The book of philosophy of Yus-Asaf is called as 'Busha' in Arabic. Busha means a religious book or Gospel. This evidence with others proves that Yus-Asaf means Ioasaph or Isaseph. This proves without an iota of doubt that the tomb belonged to visiting John, the Baptist.

We can also place here the history recorded in

Raajataranginee. The *Raajataranginee* relates the history of a holy man named Ishaana, who performed miracles. He is said to have saved the influential statesman Vazir from death on cross, and to have brought him back to life. Afterwards Vazir became the ruler of Kashmir and governed for forty-seven years. According to Kalhana, Ishaana was the last reformer in Kashmir, and lived and worked in the first century CE. This historical narration of *Raajataranginee* unveils the mystery behind the story of Issa's escape from death on cross and his miracles. It cannot be the Jesus or Issa, but some Yogee in Kashmir who did all these miracles and saved a Vazir from the death on the cross.

If the muslim sources are compared with those of *Raajataranginee* of Kalhana, one is able to conclude that Muslim sources are talking about the existence of Ishaana of *Raajataranginee* who was a miraculous man. The tomb in Kashmir belongs to Ishaana who saved a Vazir from cross and installed him (saved Vazir) as a king. That is why, Ishaana has been remembered as a Paigambar in the Muslim sources. The stories about Issa coming from west can only point out to John's coming to India and in no way it proves the presence of Jesus Christ in India.

All these evidence can only point to the fact that John disguised as Jesus visited India and went to Kashmir, spent the rest of his life time there till his death.

10

Indian Origin of Arabia

Aristotle was told by a Jewish scholar that the Jews were Hindus. This is a very important statement, but to accept this statement as true in abscence of same evidence is not proper. We must find out the evidence to prove it. We must first see who the residents of Palestine were in those days. It is important to note that Indians, who are known, as per Sanskrit sources, as the first born human beings on the globe, spread and settled over different parts of globe from time to time. This fact can be verified on the basis of the cultural, social and linguistic evidences and archaeological findings that are available to prove that the entire Europe, Asia, Africa and America was inhabited by Indians. The history of these places is the History of Indian past.[1] Palestine was also not an exception to this fact. Savarkar (2003:25) quotes Pandit Ruchiram, a member of Arya Samaj in India who, vouched to propagate Arya religion, had been to Arabia and roamed for seven years in various parts of Arabia. He has written his travelogue titled as '*Seven Years in Arabia*' in which very important information is recorded. In short, it is as follows:

1] He started on foot from Karachi. He visited various places in Baluchistan. He saw port of

---

[1] See for detail, *India the Civiliser of the World*, by Ravi Prakash Arya, International Vedic Vision New York & Indian Foundation for Vedic Science, India, 2005.

Pasni in Pakistan crowded with the shops of the Sindhi and Gujarati Hindus. They are staying there for nearly two thousand years as recorded in the history there.

2] After Iran, he visited port Gwadar which is also inhabited by Hindus for the last two thousand years. Most of them are Gujarati Hindus. Their traditions and customs are like those of Indians. Sindhi, Gujarati and Arabs are in trading.

3] At the southern coast of Arabia there is a port called as Mokalla or Mokala. Hindus are residing there for about two thousand and five hundred years. However, the trade is in hands of Indian Shia Muslims.

4] Residents of Yemen were the Hindus till the upsurge of Mohammed who established Muslim religion. Mohammed came with his followers in this province and threatened the king. He said, 'Accept me as a Paigambar and accept Muslim religion, otherwise there will be forceful conversion with bloodshed.' The king and the people were not able to defend themselves and had to bow before the Muslim invaders and embraced Islam.

5] In Syria there is a small Hindu kingdom which is governed by French. The people call themselves 'Durja'. They are very brave. Their population is about twenty to twenty-five thousand. Pandit Ruchiram and others describe them as follows: They say they are Hindus. They keep a wad of hair, shaving the whole skull. They worship idols of the Hindu Gods and Goddesses. Their religious preceptors and spiritual teachers get livelihood through religious donations. If they meet some Hindu from India they feel great happiness and they honour him. They tell, 'In the past there was fought a great war (*Mahaabhaarata* War) and after it we came here to reside'. They observe the day of their arrival in Syria as a holy, auspicious day and celebrate it. Their customs and traditions are just like the Hindus in India.

Not only Syria, the Durjas can also be located in Arabia. As per information supplied by Hindu, the Madras Daily (1940) people of Hindu community who were idol worshippers existed in Arabia for several centuries. They lived there surrounded by Muslim tribes. The people of Hindu community there spoke Arabic, and they called themselves as 'Durjas'. Their full name in Arabic was 'Davil Dal Duruj' meaning 'people of Durja'. The Durjas were divided into two notable classes. One group wore orthodox tuft and another did not. Those who did not wear the tuft were in greater number. The Durjas were worshipper of Shiva and Ganapati and they had idols installed in temples for their worship. Some shrines were actually built very much on the lines of Hindu temples in India. Many other have adopted the pattern of Mosques. In addition to the book of Pandit Ruchiram, other evidences also support this view, which are appended below.

6] Mr. Philip Smith (1879) informs that the Arabs formerly shaved their heads clean keeping a tuft of hair intact, on the crown of head, called as 'Shikha'. One great warrior in the past was named as Muthapha.

7] Dr. D.C. Oliari states in his book '*Arabia before Mohammed*' that in the Christian Patriotic literature Arabs were described as Hindus.

8] About a hundred years ago Major Wilford was told by the Hindus in India that Mecca was Hindu's holy place. In about the same period Jain people had told Dr. Buchanon that in the past, many Hindus lived in Arabia and their king Parashva Bhattaraka ruled over Mecca.

9] The fact is that prior to the advent of Islam whole of Arabia was full of the followers of Vedas and Vedic Dharma. Bardic tribute to the four Vedas by an Arab poet, Labi-bin-e-Akhtab-bin-e-Turfa as early as 2300 years before prophet Mohammed is found on page 257 of Saerul-Okul an anthology of ancient Arabic verse. That verse with a short note on the poet has been written on a column of the Yajnashaalaa in the backyard of the Lakshminarayana Temple (alias Birla Temple) on the Reading Road in New Delhi (Vedic Science: April-June, 2007).

The Arabic poem transcribed in the Roman script is as under :

aya muwarekal araj yushaiya noha minar Hind-e wa aradakallaha manyoni jail jikaratun. 1

wahalatjjali yatun ainana sahabi akha-atun jikra wahajayhi yonajjelur-raul minar HINDATUN. 2

yakuluonallaba ya ahalal araj alameen kullahum fattabe-u jikaratl VEDA hukkum malam yonajjaylatun. 3

wahowa alamus SAM wal YAJUR minallahay tanajeelan fa-enoma-ya akhiyo muttabay-an yobassheriyonajatun. 4 wa-sai-nain humaRIG-ATHAR nasayhin ka-a-khuwatun we asanat ala-udan wahowa masha-e-ratun. 5

A free English rendering of Labi's celebrated poem singing the praises of the Vedas goes like this :

1. Because Thou art the chosen of God blessed with divine knowledge enough; that knowledge which like four light-houses shone with such brilliance.

2. Through the (utterances of) Indian sages in four-fold abundance God enjoins on all humans to follow unhesitatingly.

3. The path of the Vedas with His divine precept lay down. Bursting with (divine) knowledge of SAM and YAJUR bestowed on creation.

4. Hence brothers respect and follow the Vedas guides to salvation. Two others - the RIG and ATHAR teach us fraternity.

5. Sheltering under their lustre dispels darkness till eternity.

Incidentally Labi's assertion that Arabs were initiated by a study of the Vedas in the Indian doctrine of human fraternity proves the Indian origin of civilisation in Arab countries.

In addition to these sources ancient Indian historical sources like *Mahaabhaarata, Garga Samhitaa* and *Puraanas* while narrating the history of Arab calls it Arbuda country which was founded by the Rajputs of Ketu Vamsha. Afterwards this territory was occupied by the Rajputs of Taalajanghaa clan. This state was known as Yavan after the name of Yavan, one of the heroic king of Taaljanghaa clan. Later on the word Yavan converted into Yaman. Yeman is still one of the states of United Arab Emirates. Arabi language is called a Yaavanee language in Sanskrit. (Parmar, 2004)

10.1. Indian Origin of Arabian Gods

The commonly worshipped God in Arabia and around was Shankar or Ishaana. Ishaana is one of the several names of Shiva. Therefore, wherever there was a reference to the God or Ishvara, it was to Shankar. The son of God was famous as Skanda or Kartikeya. The name 'Skanda' was in use in Arabia and around and was corrupted to Skandar and then Kandar. The famous place Canterbury in England was Kandarpuri or Skandpuri. Skanda was converted to Kandar and then in Arabic converted to Eskandar. In India, too, those who are not in touch with Sanskrit pronounce 'Skanda' as *Iskanda, Snaana* as *Isnaana, Smarana* as *Ismarana, Skula* as *Iskula.* They add 'A' or 'E' before uttering 'Ska' or any other compound word beginning with letters. We have developed this style under the Islamic influence. They said 'Snaan' as 'Asnaan' and 'Smarana' as 'Asmarana'. Therefore it is no wonder that the name 'Skanda' got converted to 'Askandar' or 'Iskandar' outside India. Skanda was the Chief General of the army of the Gods according to the *Puraanas.* Skanda was therefore accepted as the God of war. In the west Asia and regions around it, the Divine General was supposed to be Iskandar. In Persian language he was called as Sikandar. Thus Sikandar, Iskandar, Skandar were names of same Skanda or Kartikeya the son of Shankar, who was appointed as the general of army. Shankar is also known as Mahesha and Isha in the Indian literature. This Mahesha or Isha was worshipped commonly in the West Asia and the European territory nearby. This name 'Mahesha' got corrupted to Mozes. According to Cory (1876), the previous form of Moses is 'Moyeses'. Greek and other languages were close to Sanskrit, but in them the 'Visarga' took the form of 'S'. If this 'S' or 'Visarga' is removed from Moyeses, the form becomes Mozes. Mahesha (Mahesh) = Mohesh=Mozes are very close to each other. 'H' is replaced by 'Y' while other parts remained the same. In Bengal Mahesh is uttered as 'Mohesh'. Similar change occurred there and further Mohesh changed to Moyesh and Mozes. 'He' may be changed to 'Ye'. Let us notice some more similarities.

10.2. Indian habitation Surrounding Arabia

Not only Arabia, but there are evidence to prove that the people residing in many countries encircling Arabia were also Indians. To the west of Arabia are territories of Europe and Africa. To the north of Arabia are Turkestan, Russia and Siberia. To the east of Arabia are Iran, Afghanistan and Baluchistan. To the south is the sea. These are the four boundaries of Arabia. Now we shall see Indian habitations encircling Arabia.

a] **Africa** - Touching Arabia, in the continent of Africa, there are countries like Egypt, Sudan, Ethiopia (Abyssinia). These countries were inhabited by Indians. In ancient Indian historical records, South Africa is known as Shonitapur. This state was captured by the great Daitya king Bali from the people of Naagavamsha, when he was ousted by Vaaman from the kingdom of Baavala (Parmar, 2004). After *Mahaabhaarata* war, many clusters of people, who favoured Kaurvas in the war, escaped India for safer heavens and settled in Africa, Europe, eastern as well as the western parts of Asia. The *Mahaabhaarata* war occurred in 3067 BCE according to Indian historical and astronomical records (*Vedic Science*: Oct.-Dec.2006)

Let us now see about colonies of Africa, Egypt

and Ethiopia. Colonel Olcott (1881:124)) states, 'Egypt was inhabited by the Hindus at least 8000 years ago and decorated Egypt by their great culture'. According to the same author, Dr. Brugsch bey (1875), a well known archaeologist and Egyptologist and modern and reliable expert about Egypt, states, 'In the remote past unknown to the history, the Hindus from India spread and crossing many countries they came to Egypt where they settled on the banks of the river Nile. 'Nile' is a word transformed from original Sanskrit word *'Neela'*. The ancient literature of Egyptians has recorded that those people came from the God's country to settle down here. There is a carved map in the Queen's temple at Der es Bani, in Egypt. This map clearly shows that the land of the God was India. Egyptians call their previous land as 'Panta Desha' or the God's land. This has been proved by E Pococke (2004) who states, "The Sindhis from 'South India' were expert in trading and quite courageous. Those Sindhis and some Punjabi warriors went to Iran via the Arabian sea. They crossed the Red sea to enter Egypt, Nubia and Ethiopia (Abyssinia) where they colonised that land. Later some of them went further to establish in Greece.'

Pococke (2004) maintains in his history book, 'It is proved by many evidences that the Indians from the north-west India and the Himalayas went to Africa and settled there in colonies.' To prove his point, he cites following evidences:

A)   The provinces and the rivers in Greece are named after the great rivers in India.

B)   Similarly some lands are named after the cities and provinces of India.

C)   The rulers were named after Indian kings e.g. Ramesh or Ram = Rameshis.

D)   Carvings and buildings are similar to India in their grandeur and skill.

E)   Egyptian words are derived from Sanskrit words.

All these points prove that Egypt was inhabited by the Indian.

Prof. Heeren (1846) examined the skulls of Indian and Egyptian people. He was surprised to see marked similarity between the two. From that observation he has concluded that the Egyptian people were originally Hindus. He also examined social, religious and political aspects, structures, establishments, traditions and customs when he found marked resemblance between Egyptians and Indians. Therefore he concluded that Egypt was definitely colonised by the Hindus. He adds further that Ethiopia (Abyssinia) was also a Hindu land.

Sir W. Jones states (1788-1797), 'Abyssinia and India both are the countries of one extraordinary race'. Eusebius states, 'The people near Sindhu river came to Egypt and settled as a colony'. One Egyptian author named as Philostratus, quoted by Pococke (2004), says, 'Hindus were more knowledgeable than any other race and the Hindus came to colonise Egypt. There they preserved their knowledge and customs and traditions and maintained the memory of their mother land alive, told my father.' In the third century A.D. Julius Africanus had reported some information which was kept documented by Eusebius Uselius and Sincelus. Prof. Heeren has reported in his book *'Historical Researches'* that the ancient Abyssinians were the people who came from the river Abusin (an ancient name of the river Sindhu) to Africa for settlement. In the ancient era there was continuous trade between Abyssinia and India to a great extent. Colonel Tod (1820) states that the towns established near the pools of Gambia and Senegal had been given Indian names. He further states in the Asiatic Journal Part 4, quoting from a book named as 'The Second Journey of Park during 325 CE' that there is a big list of Sanskrit names given to the internal parts of Africa, and those names are still present in India in various parts. The history of India in Iran, Afghanistan and Baluchisthan is so fresh that it need not be retold.

Colonel Tod (1820) has quoted Abdul Gazi that Tamaka, the son of Ture and his colleagues established settlements in Turkestan. These people are referred to as 'Turushka' in the *Puraanas*. Turks are known as Turanians in English. About those people the *Mahaabhaarata* says that they were cursed people and their rights as heir were denied legally. Col. Tod (1820) states, 'The traditional history of Jaisalmer tells that Yadus and Balhikas reigned in Khorasan after the *Mahaabhaarata* war, and these people are called as Indo-Sythic by Greek historians. 'Many people of Kuru dynasty settled in the region from the Central Asia to the Western Asia's border. The epic *Mahaabhaarata* states about Uttara Kuru, the same are mentioned by Greek historians as 'Otoro Kurani' people. One Muslim historian states that the Hindus came first to colonise Khatha (Sarda : 2007:151).

Indians migrated outward for colonising the central Asia and then they went farther north to establish themselves in Siberia. They built its capital named as 'Vajrapur'. Shri Krishna's sons Varadamana, Saamba and Gada migrated there with many Brahmins and Kshatriyas. The elder became the king after the death of the king there. When Krishna expired, those people returned to Dwaraka, India, in condolence, as stated in the '*Hari Vamsha*'. After some period they again went back crossing the Sindhu river to Kabulisthan and onward up to Samarkand they colonised the region. In Siberia even today some of their lineage is found in pure status. Their language is also Indo-German according to 'Asia Polyglotta' authored by Klaproth (1823). The coins and stamps of the ancient Hindu kings are discovered in the Asia Minor and Turkistan. On those coins on one side there are the Moon and the Sun while on the other side there are Shiva and Nandi. The names of the Vedic deities Indra, Varuna and Naasatyau are also carved on the coins. Pure Sanskrit names are still found in the towns and villages in Asia Minor and Turkistan. The people there were named as 'Turushka' in the Puraanas.

Europe : England, Sweden, Norway, Ireland (Arya-Land), Germany, Italy, France, etc. were all inhabited by Indians. This is proved by many evidences (Arya, 2005; Sarda, 2007). We need not go into details of those evidences because it is not subject matter of this book. We have stated this as a passing remark. Similarly it is proved by Chamanlal (1940) that before Europeans entered into America, there were the Indians situated there in many states, kingdoms, nations, etc. Many evidences are shown by him to prove his thesis. In the same way, Arabia was also inhabited by the Indians. This hypothesis is not only supported by above points, but there are many other evidences to prove it. For example, marked prevalence of Sanskrit words in their language, their tradition existing even today, their dresses showing similarity with the Indian dresses, the archaeological findings, their history, stories, legends and many more such testimonies from different aspects and different fields spread all over the world show that in ancient times Indian civilisation and culture ruled the earth. Similarly there are findings that prove the Indian presence in

Arabia too. The nature of this book requires evidences to prove the presence of the Indians in Arabia and Palestine.

10.3. Indian (Tamil) Origin of Arabic

It is well known that in India there was a great dynasty famous as 'Maurya'. King Ashoka was a famous emperor from this dynasty. He had sent scholars to spread Buddhism in the western countries as well as the eastern countries. Those preachers had gone to Egypt, Syria, Palestine, Aepirus, Greece, Macidona, etc. Buddhist was a philosophical religion which was not comprehensible to the uncultured and nomadic people, because it was full of the commandments like Truth, Non-violence etc. If such nomads, uncultured people inhabited the western territories upto Greece, it was futile to preach such a high grade philosophy to them. But it was not the case. Indians were there and the Vedic religion embraced the best philosophy and ethics. Therefore it is evident that the people there were capable to learn and understand the language and concepts of Buddhist preachers. In the Christ Church, Psalm 68-31, in the common prayer 'Morians' are referred to. European scholars connected Morians to Abyssinia. But it is important to note that in the Bible those original Aramaic words are kept intact, because of their significance and auspicious nature. In its translations also, those words are kept intact. They are still present in Tamilnadu state of India, in the Tamil language, even though two thousand years have passed. These words are spoken and written in the present Tamil. Therefore, it is evident that Aramaic language is a corrupt form of Tamil. It is for this reason that the Morians mentioned in Aramaic language are the famous Mauryas of India. It is also natural that the Mauryas are mentioned in the Bible by the Indian people. There should not be any doubt in mind to accept this fact.

It is stated above that the words said to have uttered by Christ are preserved in the original form in the Bible as well as in its translations. For example, let us see here some words. In the Bible there are two words 'Korwan' and 'Korapanam', which are originally Tamil words and are corrupted in translations. In fact, these are two separate words. Korwan means the thing offered to the God or a victim offered to a deity. This word corrupted in Aramaic to 'Korbani or Kurbani'. 'Korapanam' means a thing or money kept in front of a deity with prayer. However in the Bible's translation both the words are supposed to be a thing kept for a deity. In Tamil Korapanam or Korikkapanam means the money offered to a deity in worship. Korban = Kodubbanai is also a Tamil word. It is not necessary to tell that Tamil transformed into Aramaic. A word 'Boanerjes' means 'Vaneruje' in Tamil and both these similar words mean 'Son of Thunder producer'.

When crucified Christ allegedly said, 'Eloi, Eloi, Lama Sabacthani'. These words are almost Tamil, with a little change. The original form of this sentence is 'Eloi, Eloi, Lama Sabac tha ni.' = Eloi, Eloi, Sabac Lama thani. = The Pure Tamil sentence is, 'Eloi, Eloi, Sabikka Lamada Ni'. The meaning of this sentence is 'Oh God, why are you crushing me like this ? Why do you not take me away quickly?' In the modern Tamil, the sentence as told by a Tamil person in Pune, according to Dr. P.V. Vartak, is 'Ennai, Sabic Lamada Ni'. Ennai = to me. Sabic = curse or crush. Lama = God. Da is a suffix showing triviality. Ni = you. Many such similarities may be shown. However, whatever is told is quite sufficient, but many more important and attractive words showing similar meaning can be cited.

After *Mahaabhaarata* war lot of Indian Kshatriyas who fought against Pandvas escaped India for safer heavens for the fear of being prosecuted by victorious Paandavas and went to settle outside India in the areas that were already occupied by Indians in the remote past. In Tamil as well as in Sanskrit language, 'Alla, Amma, Akka', are the names applied to the Goddess, who is the mother of this Universe. It was inevitable that these words travelled with the Indians to Arabia. In ancient Arabia and around, Shankar, Durgaa, Vishnu were worshipped as principal deities. Therefore the names of these Goddesses were abundantly used by the people there. Out of these words 'Alla' is commonly used as favourite by Muslims. Originally 'Alla' is a feminine word in Sanskrit, but Muslims use it as a masculine gender. Its meaning is supreme deity. Mohammed who introduced Muslim religion was born in a race named as 'Koresh', according to history. This race 'Koresh' constituted of people who were related to 'Kuru' dynasty or having Kurus as their kings, but they migrated from India to Arabia. Kuru dynasty is famous in the *Mahaabhaarata.* Kurus were from the race called as *'Chandra vamsha'* which means related to Moon. Therefore those 'Koresh' had a sign of the Moon on their flag. The same sign of the Moon is used by Mohammed as a sign of religion. Thus the Koresh were related to Kauravas of the Lunar dynasty.

It is pertinent here to inform that the entire humankind in ancient times was classified into solar and lunar races. These solar and lunar dynasties were called as *Soorya vamsha* and *Chandra Vamsha* respectively. Sun is also known as 'Hema' and Moon as 'Soma'. So, outside India the humankind was divided on the same Vedic pattern as Hemitic and Semitic races after the same Vedic pattern of *Soorya vamsha* and *Chandra Vamshas*. The Indian migrant from Solar race called themselves as Hemitic and from lunar race called themselves as Semitics. This division of humankind into Solar and Lunar races was based purely on astronomical grounds. In ancient times the calculation of the time of the entire world was done by Indians with Ujjain as 0^0 longitudes. Today also we have a *Mahaakaala* temple in Ujjain which signifies the Greenwich Time of ancient world. The people inhabiting to the east of Ujjain were called as solar races and to the west of Ujjain as lunar races. In fact, the dividing line between solar and lunar races was that East and West directions measured with Ujjain as the central point or 0^0 longitudes. On account of the same reason, Rama of Ayodhya was said to be Soorya Vamshee and Paandavas or Kauravas of Indraprastha and Hastinapur (Delhi) were called as Chandra Vamshee. Since Eastern direction is dominated by Sun or Soorya and Western direction is dominated by Chandra or Moon. When there is Sun shining in the East, Moon reigns over the Western horizon.

Now let us examine one more evidence which may be a bombshell to readers. Jesus Christ is not a single name. It is composed of two separate words: Jesus and Christ. Jesus is derived from a Greek word Jeshua, according to Din Farrar Kim quoted by Sarvarkar (2007:46), 'Jeshua is a form of Jeshu'. But it is not true. Jeshus is not a corruption of the name 'Shesha' or 'Sashu', it is a corruption of Jeshua. In that period, in the western countries, Jeshua and Joshua were the two forms of the same name. Many preserved it either in one form or another.

It is very meaningful to note that the legendary reports of evangelists describe governor named as

Pilate, who sentenced Jesus, calling Jesus not only as 'Jesus Christ' but as 'Jesus the Christ'. Both Jesus and Christ were the names of Sri Krishna of *Mahaabhaarat*. 'Jesus' is an English form of the Greek name 'Jeshua or Joshua'. It is usual that when a word from one language is borrowed by another language, it undergoes linguistic change or modification. Because Tamil or Aramaic were the languages of the India born of Sanskrit, it is impossible to have a name as Jeshua or Joshua in them. Therefore this corruption in Greek must be from an original Indian name. Jeshua or Joshua is the corruption of the name Keshava or Keshao. The name transformed thus - Keshava - Keshao- Keshua- Jeshua-Joshua.

Let us now consider the word Christ. Krishna (mostly spelled by Europeans as Christna or Chrisna is a Sanskrit word which is corrupted to Krishto or Krushto in Bengali as a love-word. Bengali folks always utter the name 'Kristo or Krusto or Krushto' while singing a poem in worship of the Lord Krishna. It is well known in Maharashtra that Vitthal of Pandharpur is called as Vithal or Ithal while singing a song in praise of Vitthal. In such songs pronunciation is not done clearly, but is done loosely or softly to exhibit love and affection towards the God. In Tamilnadu and even in Karnataka, the name 'Krishna' (Christna) is pronounced as 'Krista'(Christ) in a language full of love, while singing devotional songs. The term 'Krista' travelled along with Indian immigrants to the western countries. The legendary reports of evangelists also called Krisht or Christ as 'Keshao' after the name of Krishna of *Mahaabhaarata*. It is already shown that in Arabia worship of Shiva and Vishnu was popular and prevalent. Shiva was the common God to all immigrants who were basically Vaishnvites in nature. Vaishnvites in early period of their immigration had Rama as their chief Lord. The story of Old Testament bears out this fact in very explicit terms. We know that Abraham was a great personality of the Jews or the Hebrews. In fact, Abraham is said to be original person from whom Yehudis originated. In the original literature the name recorded is 'Abram'. The experts of Biblical language say that the Prefix 'Ab' in 'Abram' is a short form of the word 'Abba'. Originally the real word was 'Abbaram', which later converted to 'Abram' and then corrupted to Abraham. Some prefixes of present language were suffixes in ancient era. For example, Kanhaiyya = Ayya Kannu, Kannu Swami = Swami Kannu, Appa Kutti= Kutti Appa = Kuttippa. In the same fashion Biblical Abbaram was originally Ramabba>Ramappa, meaning Sri Rama, famous in the *Raamaayana*. How does it happen? This question may be answered in the following pages.

10.4. Indian (Tamil) Origin of Aramaic

It is already stated that the language of Palestine was Aramaic and it was a version of Tamil language. In the word 'Aramaic', the suffix 'aic' is from European languages. If we remove that suffix, there remains only 'Aram'. 'Aram' itself is a short corrupt form of the word 'Arvam'. Arvam can be located in Tamil language. It means that the language Arvam is Tamil itself. 'Arvam' is the other name of Tamil. Therefore the Aramaic language of Vaishnavites in Arabia was Tamil. The word 'Arav' got corrupted to 'Arab'. The New Testament was first written in Greek language and then translated into English. There were three languages running in Palestine. One was the regional language 'Aramaic', second was the royal language of Italy, because at that time Palestine was ruled by Rome. Third language was Greek which was honoured as a scholarly language of knowledge or literature. It shows that Apostles of the Krishnanity (Christianity) in the west must have preached in the local Aramaic language as well as the scholarly language, Greek. The same must have been recorded in both the languages as a precious literature. Therefore, the Tamil uttering assigned to the Palestinian Krishna (Christ) by the Apostles must have been recorded in Greek language in the New Testament. The Roman language was also not excluded to record the words assigned to Jesus the Christ. The New Testament written in Greek must have been converted to Roman language too, because it was a royal language.

10.5. Indian Borrowings in Chaldean's Aramaic Language

Many Indian articles have been discovered in archaeological excavations near Mesopotamia, Syria etc. This proves the presence of Indian people in those places in the ancient times. Palestine and Arab were dominated by Indians who hailed from southern parts of India i.e. Tamilnadu. Tamil language assumed a new form in the Arab as Aramaic language. Aramaic was a corrupt form of Tamil language and the words Yahva or Yahava and Jahva or Jahava travelled there through those Tamil Indians immigrants. In the Bible, we find Arvam or Tamil names or titles in the same form or in a little bit transformed form. Some are illustrated below:

1) Achar = Acharya
2) Azaria   = Acharyayya
   Ayya is a suffix to a name in Tamil
3) Obadiah   = Upaadhyaaya
4) Caleb = Kalappa
5) Nagash = Naaga, cobra
6) Nehamiah= Nahamayya
7) Naamah   = Nahamma.
8) Merari = Murari

9)   Meremoth= Marimutthu
10) Shallam   = Selem = Selemia
11) Ezara   = Eshwara= Ishwara.
12) Isaiah   = Ishayya= Isha + Ayya.
13) Sheva   = Shiva.
14) Shamgar = Shankar
15) Sheshan   = Shesha
16) Jeshaih = Sheshayya
17) Jeshab, son of Ishwara = Sheshappa.
18) Maeseiah = Mahashaya.
19) Rhoda   = Radha
20) Rachab = Rajappa.
21) Simon   = Sheeman=Shreeman
22) Carmil = Carai Malai= Mountain on the
seashore.
23) Tabor   = Deopuram (name of a city).
24) Ramoh = Rampur
25) Ramiah = Ramayya.
26) Khilaphat   = Kulapati.
27) Sarasen= Shoorasen
28) Muhajarin= Mahacharana. This is a name
     given to the people who left Mecca with
     Mohammad.
29) Mufti   = Mukhapati = Chief of men.
30) Mahammad= Maha+Mati.= wise.
31) Kouros = Krishna

11

Indian Origin of Hebrews

Having revisited Jesus the Christ, it becomes imperative to take a retrospective view of the scenario of Palestine Before Christian Era.

It is said that the original person from whom Yehudis originated is Abraham. The God exhibited himself before Abraham in the form of Fire. It is recorded in the history that the Divine Fire was called 'Jehowa'. In the *Rigveda*, Agni the fire is called '*Jahva*'. '*Jahvo Agnih*' (*Rigveda*, 7.6.5). This evidence shows that the people there were fire worshippers. Later the word 'Jahva' was transformed to 'Jehowa'.

Israel is a corrupt from of 'Ijrail'. Ijra or Ijja is the origin of that word. Ijja is a corrupt version of the word 'Yaja'.

The Bible records many conversions of the word 'Hibru'. They are - Habiru, Habiri, Hapiru, Apiru. These words appear to be corrupt form of the basic word 'Abhira'. The Abhira people are famous in the epic *Mahaabhaarata*. These Abhiras defeated Arjuna after the death of Sri Krishna and abducted away many Yadava ladies. The descendants of those Abhira people are Hibru or Habiri. It is also a well known fact that the Yadavas became arrogant and behaved unscrupulously, troubled good people, so Lord Krishna had to take part in killing them. Some of those astrayed Yadavas also ran away from

India towards the west and settled first in Egypt followed by Palestine. All of them were not astrayed. Those who were gentlemen remained attached to the original Vedic religion and customs and they performed pious deeds. Probably these pious people from the Vedic tradition gathered together to form a cult called as Ishaana or Essene. Here it may be pointed out that John the Baptist belonged to the cult of Essenes.

It is also a fact that various classes of Kshatriyas travelled to many parts of Europe and Asia after *Mahaabhaarata* war because the parts of Europe, the Middle East and Egypt were the part of Greater India (called as Bharat Varsha) itself then and the Vedic culture was in vogue there too. Hence, those people cannot be said to be different from the Indians.

Abhiras were originally Yadavas. It is wrong to assume that they remained confined only to Punjab, Sindh etc. The famous Yadavas from the Maharashtra are the descendants of those ancient Yadavas, among whom great Krishna was born. It is quite possible that those Yadavas spread upto Sri Lanka. As Yadavas spread from Gujarat to Lanka, people from various other parts of India went out to settle down distant parts of Greater India. Tamils also migrated into Jerusalem and Arab countries. The late Mr. Krishna T. Jaitley (Sarvarkar, 2007) has published a nice research paper '*Who were Abhiras*? in which he has discussed many points and has proved that the Kshatriyas specially known as Yadavas after the name of Sri Krishna's clan spread all over the world.

Around Jerusalem, there was habitation of Indians in ancient era. This fact is supported by a postal stamp printed by Iraq in 1989, on which is printed a picture of Sri Krishna, and below a line was published as 'Mosul Spring Festival'. This evidence shows that Sri Krishna is still in memories there, though 5000 years have lapsed since his death.

It has already been pointed out above that Indians settled in Palestine after migrating from Tamilnadu of South India and they were Tamil in race.

11.1. Linguistic Evidence

Let us first examine linguistic evidence. Like other countries, Arabia also possesses a lot of Sanskrit words as well as Tamil words. The evidence is here : When Jesus was crucified, he has been shown exclaiming some words which are preserved carefully. He was made to utter, *'Talith Kumi Eloi, Eloi, Lama Sabaktheni'*. Its meaning is 'Oh God, why are you crushing me like this?' This has already been explained.

It may be pointed out here that during that period Aramaic language was in common currency in Palestine. Aramaic is a word transformed from a Sanskrit word Arvam, as already pointed out, Tamil language was known as Arvam. In those times, among Jews there was a difference between a scholar and an ordinary man. Scholars were called Pharisees. They used to tell their *'Gotra'* after the name of an Indian sage, like Braahmans in India. It is for this reason that the Jew Pandits told Aristotle that they belonged to genealogies of Indian sages. Later they forgot the speciality of *Gotra* and began telling that they are descendants of Philosophers. [*Gotras* are now forgotten even in India].

It is stated above that Arabic language was known as Arvam. Let us find out its roots. The Jews are called as Hebrews. Hibru is a corrupt form of Habiru. Habiru is derived from Abhira. 'A' in Tamil means cattle. 'Bheera' means brave. The word 'Abheera' got converted to 'Ameer' or 'Avir' in the local language there. According to natural conversions in language 'Amir' became 'Aribh' and then 'Arib' or 'Arab'. The Jews were known as 'Habiri' and also 'Khabiri'. These are the original words there. If we delve deep to find out how these words came up, we find that both these words are different from each other, but were applied to the same race. 'Khabiri' is the word arisen out of geography, while 'Habiri' arose from race, according to experts. In Arabia and Palestine, Tamil people had settled. (This will be proved later with different evidence). Those Tamil people were from banks of the river Kaveri. The river Kaveri, which is reputed in Tamilnadu, is one of the most celebrated rivers, out of the seven ranked as the great river Ganga. During a bath usually these seven names of the rivers are uttered as a Mantra. These seven are Ganga, Yamuna, Godavari, Saraswati, Narmada, Sindhu and Kaveri. Thus river Kaveri was also supposed to be great and so the people residing at its banks mark it as their speciality and they identified themselves with Kaveri. The name 'Kaveri' corrupted to 'Khabiri' according to some experts. Those Abhiras or Yadavas were dark in complexion. It is famous that Lord Krishna was also dark in complexion. The dark complexion is called in Sanskrit as 'Shyama'. This 'Shyama' colour of Yadavas got corrupted to 'Shema' and then in English got converted to Semaite. Semaite means about Shyama coloured or about Shem people. It is no wonder that the Greeks, according to their style of language, called the residents of Palestine and region upto Cyprus, as Shyamites or Semitics.

One more interesting evidence in support of Tamil origin of Hebrews can be given as under. The word used in the Hebrew Bible for peacock is 'tukki'. 'Tukki' is a corrupt form of Tamil word 'tokei', the name of peacock. Also the ape or monkey in Hebrew is 'koph' which again is the corrupt form of Sanskrit 'kapi'.

11.2. Indian Origin of Jewish Bible

There are many legends in the Bible. The similarity of words is recognized by the legends. From the similarity of words we can examine the names and stories also. Let us examine it here. Abraham was a great personality of the Jews or the Hebrews. In the original literature the name recorded is 'Abram'. The experts of Biblical language say that the Prefix 'Ab' in 'Abram' is a short form of the word 'Abba'. Originally the real word was 'Abbaram', which later converted to 'Abram' and then corrupted into Abraham. As already highlighted, some prefixes of present language were suffixes in ancient era. For example, Kanhaiyya = Ayya Kannu, Kannu Swami = Swami Kannu, Appa Kutti= Kutti Appa = Kuttippa. In the same fashion Biblical Abbaram was originally Ramappa, who was Sri Rama, famous in the *Raamaayana*. Let us examine this fact.

The wife of Biblical Abraham, according to a Biblical story, was taken away by Philistine. This Philistine means Pulastiyan.

According to the *Raamaayana,* Ravana was Paulastya,i.e. descendant of a sage Pulist. In the same sense the word Philistine is used in the Bible. A friend of Abraham according to the Bible was 'Aner'. Aner is a corrupt form of the word derived from 'Vaanara'. This Vaanara was Hanumaana. The Bible is not a book of stories, so the whole story could not be reported in it. But whatever is stated in short points to Rama-Ravana.

The word 'Sri' in Sanskrit converts to Tiru, Thiru or Siri in Tamil language. It is applied to the name of a city Tirupati in Tamilnadu province and that style has gone to the west Asia. Tirupati houses a famous Tirupati temple dedicated to Sri Krishna. This is considered one of the leading holy places in India. Thus Tirupati was a habitate of Lord Krishna's devotee or followers. When these followers of Krishna (called as Yadus in North India) spread away from that city, they honoured their original habitat, that first city developed by their ancestors as the holy place. Therefore they called it 'Siri Salem'. Probably Sri Shailam got converted into Siri Salem. Later Siri Salem converted into Jerusalem, which became popular. There is valley near Salem, they named it as Shaveh (Shaiva or Shiva Dari). In Madras near Salem there was a place named as Shiva Pet. It is still present there. So it is concluded that Salem, Siri, Sri Salem and Shevadari were the names of places originally in Tamilnadu area, which travelled to west Asia along with the migrating Indians.

In the Bible,'*Geeta*' finds its mention. In the English or European script there is no 'T' (as in Teheran, or Sanskrit words Tadaaga, Tanu, Tara, Tilak, Teertha, Turanga, Taila, Toya, Taulam etc.). The class of 'T' like t, th, d, dh, is not present in the Roman script. Therefore for 'T' is used and for ▢'D'is used. In Sanskrit 't' is replaced many times by 'd'▢▢For example, 'tat'>'tad'▢▢Therefore, '*Geeta*' was written as 'Gheeda'. Due to the difference in the language and the script and due to the poverty of syllables and letters other scripts cannot write Sanskrit words correctly. In the Bible it is often stated that 'now I shall quote some parables from *Gheeda*'. It is similar to the fashion of Sanskrit where sayings of sages are quoted stating, '*Iti Uktam*". *Gheeda* means *Geeta* as shown above. Therefore those quotations from *Gheeda* must form the part of the *Geeta*. There is no book named as '*Gheeda*' in Europe or the west Asia or Palestine. Thus the parables are the quotations of the great personalities or from the books of some secret knowledge or from the teachings of the *Geeta*. In other words, it shows that the person who told the Bible was also acquainted with the *Geeta*, and he preached its teachings to his followers. From this information and the similarities between the words, any straightforward man will admit that the *Geeta* is retold in the Bible. Some Tamil words like *Matala*, *Patela*, *Mashala*, etc. are found recorded in the Bible and their meanings tally with the Tamil sense. Therefore we have to conclude that *Gheeda* means *Geeta*. It is not necessary to go into further details.

In the Old Testament there is a reference to a book of Joshua, where a story of Jasher, five kings of Jash and their war is recorded. To whom does this story refer to? Because Palestine was inhabited by Indians, this story might have travelled there, from Indian *Puraana*, along with the Indian settlers. There are some corrupt words in Latin transformed from their original language, for example, 'Church' from 'Karka', 'Cheri' from 'Keri', 'Surukka' from 'Kurukka', 'Joshua' from 'Jeshua' etc. 'Jeshua' is a word transformed from 'Keshua' which is a corrupt form of the word 'Keshao' or 'Keshava'. In the Old Testament there are words like 'Og' and 'Makkedah'. 'Og' is told to be a giant and 'Makkedah' a king. This 'Og' means 'Aghasura' and 'Makkedah' means 'Magadha Desha (Country ruled by Jarasandha during *Mahaabhaarata* period).

Let us now think about 'Jasher' which means 'of Jash'. In Tamil 'W' transfers to 'Y'. For example, 'Vyankappa' becomes 'Yankappa'. Many times 'Y' is replaced by 'J', i.e.'y'='j'. For example, *Yajna* becomes *Jajna*. *'Yogee '* converts into *'Jogee'*. In the same manner, 'Yash' convert to 'Jash', and 'Yash' finds its origin into 'Vyaasa'. Thus the original word was 'Vyaasa', the name of the famous sage who wrote the epic *Mahaabhaarata*. Therefore, the story of the five kings in the book of 'Jash' was the story of five Paandavas written by the sage Vyaasa in the book of *Mahaabhaarata*. The war was fought between Paandavas and Kauravas. Jeshua, mentioned in it, is Keshava (Keshao) or Krishna. 'Og' is 'Aghasura' and 'Makkedh' is 'Magadha Desh' of Jarasandh. Thus, if we search the origin of the words and their corrupt forms, we find many Indian historical references from *Puraanas* and Indian personalities quoted in the Old Testament. But we must point our finger to a definite evidence, for our satisfaction. These references and stories are the abridgements of those taken by the originally settled Indians in that region of Arabia and Palestine. *'Laakshaagriha'*, the inflammable house made of *Laakshaa* built by Kauravas for burning Paandavas, is also found in the Old Testament.

Yet another evidence is cited by Sarvarkar (2007:41). The Sanskrit words *Hastin* and *Hasti* are written in Pali as *Hattin* and *Hatti*. Hittites are mentioned in the Bible, and its corrupt form 'Hatti' is found engraved in the west Asia. The Hattians are known as ancient people who inhabited the 'land of Hatti' in present-day central part of Anatolia, Turkey, noted at least as early as the empire of Sargon of Akkad ca. 2300, until they were christened ca. 2000-1700 BC as Hittites. These Hattis or Hattians or Hittites were none else but the people of Hastinapur.

It shows that the Hettite kings mentioned in the Old Testament were the kings of Hastinapura. The word 'Hastin' got converted to 'Hattin' and its adjective became 'Hettite'. In the New Testament the word 'Kouros' is present. It is a transformation of 'Krishna'. There is no doubt that it refers to Krishna. The present author came across a Jewish scholar from Orlando named as Bhakti Anand Goswami (2000) who called himself as a Vaishnva master, a Catholic Monk and an expert on ancient religions. In thirty years, he has studied over 2000 Theophoric (God-Bearing) names and over 5000 sacred, forms of symbols from Vaishnava-related religious traditions in the pre-Christian era. Tracing additional inter-disciplinary evidence from Greek, Hebrew, Egyptian and other sources back to pre-historic settlements in each region, he sorts out religious complexities and clarifies exactly how various traditions in East and West are historically related to the worship of Hari or Vasudeva. The Biblical deity Eli-Yahu, Greek Heli-Us and Egyptian Hor-Us all denote Indian God 'Hari' in one sense or the other. He further proves in his thesis that Rhoda and Kouros of Bible are nothing else but the Radha and Krishna of Bharat. For example, the figures of Radha (Rhoda) and Krishna (Kouros) depicted in Jewish tradition has been illustrated by Goswami as under:

Fig. 8 : Rhoda and Kouros
Source : Goswami (2000)

Similarly Heri, Heli and Eli are nothing else but the Hari of Bharat. Through his 30 years of research, he has come across astounding results that East or West there is one Vaishnava-related religious tradition with one God-head, Vishnu (Hari) incarnated as Rama and Krishna in the East and depicted in the West variously as Heli, Heri, Kuruos to add Abram and Christ to this list of Catholic Monk. It is shown above that the name 'Vyaasa' has taken the form of 'Jash' in Palestine. The same word is present in Arabic language. The names 'Yasser' and 'Yasir' transmuted from Vyasa are usual in Arabia.

Inspite of the Indian roots of Yehudis and Christians, the contents of the Old Testaments do not fit properly in Indian philosophy and therefore some may doubt about its Indian Origin. Indians, too, will not accept the Old Testament as their religious book. Others also will not agree with it.

What is the reason? If the Jews were Indians, why their religious books do not show Indian roots? This question must be answered.

11.2.1. Why Bible of Jews does not exhibit its Indian Origin?

The old religious book of the Jews is not available now in pure form. The reason is that around 587 BCE a Babylonian king Nebuchadnezzar invaded and conquered Palestine and surrounding regions. He destroyed the religions there. The Jews were totally destroyed in Palestine. Nobody knows what the religion of that king and his people was. But it is certain that it must be different from the Jews. If it was not so then they would not have destroyed the Jews and their religion. About a century later king Cyrus of Persia and Iran smashed the empire of Babylon and relieved the Jews. The Jews were now allowed to go to Palestine. In the mean time the Persians had relation with Jews, of course like donor and recipient. Therefore religious attitudes of the Jews were impressed by the Parsees. The Persians allowed them revive their religion. Naturally, it is evident that the Persians believed in revival of the Jewish religion. The revived Jewish religion might have contained many aspects of the Persian religion. This is not the proper place to discuss this issue here. We have to be satisfied with points accepted by history. Madame H.P. Blavatsky (1877-1889), a famous Theosophist, has presented the same fact openly in her books. Therefore it seems that the revived religious books of the Jews are not like the old ones, but are changed to a great extent under the influence of the Parsian religion. The Romans conquered Palestine when their emperor destroyed Jerusalem and banned the Jews to come near it. At that time the Jews spread all over the world, so different opinions, customs and traditions from different countries entered their religion and broke their unity. Due to all these reasons, the rewritten Old Testament doesn't contain original philosophy. For example, the '*Karma Siddhaanta*' and 'Rebirth theory' the main pillars of Vedic religion were present in Jews, too, as evident from some of their books like '*Wisdom of Solomon*' etc. However, the same is not attested in the Old Testament. Therefore, the Jewish religion could not survive in its pure and original form, it turned out to be the distorted one.

When the Jews suffered like this, there was one Essene cult, which in a way, preserved Indian ethical values in a secret way, remaining unattached to the surroundings, maintaining link with the ancient tradition and religion. In other parts of Arabia, Indian values were preserved to some extent, but that, too, was not in pure form, because of absence of any intercourse with India. Thus this was the state of the Jewish religion.

11.3. Indian Origin of Traditions in Palestine

An English word 'widow' is similar to Latin 'Vidua' born of Sanskrit '*Vidhvaa*' and Greek 'Cherai'. The Greek word 'Cherai' means a widow having no support of anybody. In Tamil a support less widow is called as 'Kurai'. There is marked similarity between 'Kurai' and 'Cherai'. Apostles constituted mostly of Tamil speaking Indian immigrants had prepared some rules for those who are to be appointed as preachers or Bishops in the cult of Krisht /Christ. The rules go like this:

1] The widows having support and those who are willing to consecrate their lives for the service of the God, should be supported by the church.

2] The church should not support those who receive support from some of their relatives.

3] She is a real widow who has full control over her mind and observes total celibacy, who has renounced the bondage of the world and family and who has consecrated her life for the service of the God. Only such widows should be appointed by churches as their servants.

[4] (a) One who is above the age of sixty years,

(b) Who has undergone a strict test of mind control,

(c) Who is well known in people as a virtuous and pious lady, are to be taken as servants of the churches. Young widows should never be taken as servants of the church or a maid servant of the God, because they may, in future, like to remarry and they may be seduced by public. They may not be able to control their mind; therefore they should not be taken as ascetics. On the contrary they should be allowed to remarry and enter into family life. Those old widows who were able to concentrate their mind on the God were allowed to be the maid servants of the God and become an ascetic, to live in churches. The tradition of this kind of maid servants of the God originated in India. At present it has taken a wicked form, but it was not so in the past. In the past, those who renounced the worldly pleasures of their own wilfully and tried hard to please the God sacrificing the whole life, were supposed to be the real maid servants of the God. On the other hand, some parents or relatives abandoned their daughters in young age to serve the God, without their consent or approval. That was not good. The first type of a servant of the God is respectable but the second type will not keep control over her mind and may get astray. Hence this second type is objectionable. Therefore, the forcibly made God servants are not true God servants. Those offered their lives themselves to the God with proper and full control over their mind are the true servants of God and only they earn respect in society. Hoping this, some rules about the servants of God were framed by the immigrant Indians. Even then in churches, all servants of Gods were not old in age and some young women had renounced the world in true sense and became servants of God and stayed in churches. In India, the custom was to tonsure, to cut all hair of the head of widow just like Samnyaasins do. On the other hand, some young ladies like Meerabai became servants of the God wilfully without tonsuring hair and attained authority in the spiritual field. The same tradition of the Hindus was picked up in Buddhists and Christian cults.

11.4. Indian Origin of Jewish Customs and Traditions

From the foregoing discussion, it can undoubtedly be proved that the Aramaic language was similar to that of Tamil language of India, as verified from the similarities of the words. This evidence along with others proves that the residents of Palestine and that of Arabia were south Indians. Had the Arabia and the countries around it been inhabited by the Indians, then there would have been some similarity, even at present, between Indians and the people of Arabia as far as the traditions and customs are concerned. Let us verify the facts.

Commenting on this issue a French author, Louis Jacolliot (1876) observes thus, "The manners and customs of Judea so strongly recall those of India, as of themselves to remove all doubt that might remain as to the colonization of the ancient world by emigrations from India".

One French Sojourner De La Coquinerie had travelled in India and had resided particularly in Pondicherry and Bengal for five years. He was surprised to see a marked similarity between the traditions of the Jews recorded in the Christian religious books and those of the Hindus in India. He was careful enough to record this fact in his book written after returning to Europe. He travelled in the seventeenth century CE. It is reported in the Illustrated Weekly, dated 25th April 1926, a Times of India publication (Sarvarkar, 2003:50). Reverend K. R. Gopal Achari was originally a Hindu Brahmin, but later he accepted the Christian faith and became a Father-Preceptor. He lived three hundred years later than De La Coquinerie. He has written in the *'Social Reformer'* dated 17th November 1923 that 'I am studying the Bible deeply for last ten years. I was highly amazed to read a Leviticus of the Bible. In this book are recorded all the customs and traditions followed by the ancient Jews in Palestine and those traditions and customs are almost the same as my mother observed at home before I became a Christian. It was a matter of great surprise to me. My family was highly religious and orthodox. I was dumbfounded to see the religious traditions and customs of the Jews in Palestine similar to those of the Hindus in India. Why should there be any similarity between the traditions and customs, rules and regulations of two different religions, at two different places? How this happened? In Malabar state, the Hindu ladies used to get up at dawn on Fridays and painted the utensils, pots, frames of doors etc. with red colour. There is a commandment to the Jews in Exodus 12, in parts 7 and 8, to paint utensils and frames of doors with the blood of a lamb. This commandment travelled to Arabia along with the Indian immigrants from Malabar state of India (Sarvarkar, 2003:50).

Jesus the Christ is said to have told Nicodemus that a second birth is essentially and inevitably required to seek entry in the Gods realm. It is well known that in India the educated are supposed to have born twice, 'Dvija'. It is a custom to perform a Vidhi (Sanskaara) of Upanayana, a religious rite before attaining the age of twelve years. Education is supposed to be the second birth. The first birth is only physical (from the mother) while this second birth is cultural or mental or psychical (from a Guru). This rite is performed by Brahmanas, Kshatriyas, Vaishyas, as well as Shudras and after this ceremony they are called as 'Dvija', twice born. This Indian concept of Dvija-hood, twice born, also transferred to the west along with Indian immigrant and so was attributed to the Jesus. How & why the Jews as well as Indians did not allow admixture of others (varnasankara) with them. Varnasankara has been disapproved even in Geeta. According to both, admixture of races may prove fatal and ruinous to them. Why this similarity in the two and where did it come from? If one goes through the Old Testament, he can attest there the shadow of social arrangement of four Varnas, as found in India. The reason is clear that the Jews had migrated from India to the western countries.

G.D Savarkar (2003) narrates one of his memoirs as:

'When I was ill, I had to be in Mumbai in connection with a treatment from a dispensary of N. Powel & Co. Dr. Joshi was treating me for my foot and abdominal ailments by electricity. At that time an old Jewish person also used to be there in connection with his treatment. We

both discussed many political and other issues. During the discussion, once an issue of minorities in India came up. He said, 'We Jews never find India an alien land, rather India is their homeland'. I could not believe him at that time and questioned, 'The original place of the Jews is Palestine, then how do you have claim for India?' He retorted, 'We Jews are originally Indians. We migrated outside India and settled in Palestine and countries around it. In due course of time, we got alienated from each other. Of course, at that time I did not realise the truth in his statement due to lack of information. Long after that incident, when I had reliable information about the Jews, I tried to contact him, but all in vain. I was convinced that whatever he was talking then was true. What I found unconvincing at that time appears now a true fact.'

Let us now compare some more traditions and customs of west Asia with India. GD. Savarkar (2003:75) quotes a book titled as *'The Holy Land '* from a series namely *'Peoples at Many Land series '*, published by A & C Black London, there is a description of the people inhabiting the west Asia, which is exactly similar to those of Indians. Here are cited some similarities of the traditions and customs between India and Palestine.

1] Houses of farmers of Palestine and districts of Andhra (India) are exactly similar, having flat, horizontal roofs.

2] The customs of rolling the mattress after getting up from sleep in the morning and spreading out a 'Chatai' to welcome a guest are same in both places, i.e. among the Indians and the Arabs particularly in Palestine.

3] In ancient era, the grain was stored in special pits in the middle class and higher class houses called as 'Balada', by the Indian. The same type of pits for storing grains are present in Palestine. These pits called in Marathi as 'Balada'. They are named as 'Kulukkai   or Kulumi' in Tamil.

4] For burning fire at home, sticks and wood is collected by ladies from forests, in India as well as in Palestine.

5] Filling water in vessels and carrying water-vessels on heads one above another in a row is a special style of the Indian ladies.

Fig.9
Source : Savarakra, 2003

Similarly their another style is to hold water vessel on the waist with the help of arm and forearm and a small vessel of water and a metal cup of water is held in hand. Both these styles are visible among the West Asian ladies. Ladies in other countries do not use this style at all. This peculiar similarity is a proof to hold that Palestinian women were originally the south Indians. See fig.9.

6] Use of a grinding wheel of stone rotated by

hands to powder grains is common to both the countries. See fig.10.

Fig. 10
Source : Savarkar, 2003

7] In the above mentioned book (*Peoples at Manay land Series*) there are pictures of women folk in which the ladies are shown carrying water vessels on their heads (Fig.9) and their peculiar sitting style while grinding flour (Fig.10). These styles are the same as those of the Indian ladies.

8] To prepare cakes of cow-dung and to wash clothing on the river banks with salty earth or soil is also common to both the ladies, Indian and Palestinian.

9] It is important to note that in India as well as in Palestine, there is a tradition to convert butter into Ghee, known as clarified butter before its use.

10] There is a common practice in both the countries to wash hands before and after taking meals, and to use right hand for taking meals.

11] It is important to note that many Indian women smoke tobacco and same holds true in case Palestinian women.

12] In India, God's name is invoked before taking meals. The same custom prevails in Palestine.

13] A picture of a plough seen in the above mentioned book is exactly the same as that of the Indian plough.

14] While working in forest, Indian women workers tie a cloth to some trees and make their children sleep in it. The same style is seen in Palestine. See figure 11.

Fig.11
Source : Savarkar, 2003

15]   Methods to pull down fruits like tamarind, mangoes etc from trees are common to both the countries.

16]   Species of dogs in Palestine are same as those in India. Indians might have carried their dogs along with them while immigrating palestine and other places.

Fig. 12
Source : Savarkar, 2003

17] Houses in Palestine are strong like small forts
     and are not easily accessible. Similar were the
     houses in ancient India.

18] In Arabia like that of India there is a strong
     belief that one must be loyal and faithful to
     the salt and milk of one's host. Disloyalty to
     the salt and milk is taken to be great sin.

Fig. 12
Source : Savarkar, 2003

19] To carry small kids on back is a fashion with both, the Indian women (See fig.12) as well as Arabian. A little grown up children are carried on shoulders by the Indian males; the same fashion is current in Arabia too. (See fig.12)

20] To throw a stone by a catapult or a sling is a

style   present in both India and Arabia.

Many more such similarities can be cited; but these are sufficed to prove that Indians inhabited Arabia.

11.5. Lost Religion of the Jews

Actually, the race, religion and the land of the Jews were trampled by the unjust feet of foreign invaders. The traditions and customs of the Jews were lost in Yerusalem or Jerusalem. Due to these invasions, the Jews had to excape their country for safer heavens on the globe. It is described that after their merging with others the Jews became Gentiles or Anacharyes which means they lost their culture. This word 'Anacharyes' is a corruption of the original Sanskrit word 'Anaachaaree'. The Jews supposed themselves as pious and pure like the Hindus and did not share food with non-Jews. They never married outside their race. But after maraud by invaders, they lost their piety and sacredness, they lost their culture also and so they became Anacharyes, behaved improperly, badly. The word 'Anaachaaree' and its true meaning was not understood so that it got corrupted to form the term 'Anacharyes' and spelt like that in the Roman script. In the Roman empire when Christianity became the royal religion and was accepted all over, it was supposed to be a political crime to re-admit   the Jewish religion. Christians horribly destroyed the religious books of the Jews. Between 1242 and 1247 CE, the Talmud collection of books of the Jew religion were brought to Paris in cart-loads and were burnt there openly. The Christians assaulted the Jews so terribly and perpetuated cruelty on them so inhumanly that the Jews had to forego their very religious rites. Their original language (Tamil) could not survive. This total loss was so effective that the Jews doomed physically, mentally, psychically and intellectually. They were displaced from their nationality and were settled in other countries so that they forgot their original, pure religion. Hence, the form of their original ancient religion became perverted and faint, but still it lingered in their minds. Thus, a distorted form of their religion is seen at present.

In India, various races of the Hindus and various persons mark various signs on their body, on the fore-head, wrist, arms, neck etc. For example, a leaf of a tree or a metal etc. is marked. Some wear a ring around the wrist or arm or neck. The Lingayats hold a Lingam on the forehead and wear a metal Lingam around the neck. Twice born, *Dvijas*, wear a sacred thread and also necklace of beads, Rudraaksha, Bhadraaksha, Tulasi, crystal etc. The Hindus know very well the specialities and use of those marks and signs; but the Europeans and other non-Hindus do not understand the importance and specialities and meanings of those symbols, because they have forgotten their original form and are now entangled in new or distorted moulds and concepts. They feel that those marks are for warding off the perils, evils and inauspicious things. The original figure of the Judaism is totally lost. Ornamented with foreign culture, the people forgot the essence of the Judaism. The Judaism is reformed using the distorted concepts present in Greek and Roman literature and is brought forward, therefore it is highly difficult to realise the essence of Judaism. Even then whatever form and figure of the Judaism is faintly visible now can be retraced to some extent to its original form, and find its meaning, if we cross check its similarities with the Hindu traditions and customs.

The Pharisees were at various times a political party, a social movement, and a school of thought among Jews, who were not different from the

Braahmanas of India. They were the first to colonise Palestine and they wore round their necks a mark of 'Tefillah'. What was this 'Tefillah'? 'Tefillah' is singular while 'Tefillin' is plural. In western religious literature the plural 'Tefillin' is often used. 'Tefillin' was used to prepare *Yajnopavita* or sacred thread. In India, in the remote past '*Darbha*' (a kind of grass) was used, after weaving, as a sacred mark. This view is supported by Bodhaayana's writings. Even at present, during auspicious celebrations *Darbha* is tied to the sacred thread, symbolising the old tradition, by the Hindus. *Darbha* is tied on wrist also as '*Pavitraka*' which means sanctifier or purifier. In Palestine region, *Darbha* type of grass is called 'Tefillah'. *Yajnopavita* cannot be prepared by a single *Darbha* or Tefillin, we have to use many Tefillin to weave *Yajnopavita*. Therefore the plural word Teffillin is used. Like *Darbha*, '*Tila*' or sesamum must have also been referred to in the Bible, because 'Tila' is used inevitably by Indians in their sacred rites. At that time, in Palestine Indians wer dewelling, as such the importance of sesamum was natural in the religious rites there. Therefore, '*Tila*' must have been mentioned in the Bible. This expectation is fulfilled because in the Bible a word 'Dil' has often appeared as an original word in some religious rituals. This word 'Dil' was not properly understood. If we see the similarity in pronunciation of 'Til' and 'Dil' along with its inevitability in religious functions in the Hindu traditions and the Biblical traditions, it appears clear that 'Dil' is a corrupt form of 'Til'. The country where the Hero of this book was residing was Palestine and it was inhabited, along with Arabia, by Indians. Clearchus also said that Jews were immigrants from India (Ramaswamy Iyer, 1926). To further prove this fact, the following evidences are furnished from Arabia and Palestine :

1] There was a practice of writing verses from Torah and bind it on the Phylacteries or a *Yajnopavita*.

2] It was a custom among the Jews to placed Phylacteries above the forehead, with the strap going around the head and over the shoulders just like the Indians place *Yajnopavita*.

3] It was a practice in the Jews to place Phylacteries on the upper arm, and the strap wrapped around the arm hold in hand and recite Torah command in the morning and in the evening. This practice is similar to the Brahmanic style of reciting the *Gaayatree Mantra* in the morning and in the evening holding *Yajnopavita* in hand. This is alike *Sandhyaa-Vandana* of Indians.

4] Phylacteries were held in high respect.

5] The Jews believed that even the Gods wore Phylacteries. All the Hindu Gods do wear *Yajnopavita*.

6] It was a custom among the Jews to take oath holding Phylacteries in hand. Similar is a custom among the Hindus.

7] The Jew ladies did not wear Phylacteries. The Hindu ladies do not wear *Yajnopavita*.

8] Christ is described to give secret *Mantra* while initiating his disciples and the *Mantra* was supposed to be kept secret, like the Hindus. The Hindus keep their *Mantra*, *Gaayatree* or any other, secret. Initiation of all *Mantras* is kept secret in the Hindus.

9] The present way of Baptism is corrupt, but in the beginning, during initiation, milk mixed with honey was offered to disciples. This is a corrupt form of Hindu practice of offering *Panca-Gavya*,

the five products of a cow, at the time of
Upanayana. At that ancient time there were six
thousand Pharisees (Braahmanas) spread in
Judia. In Jerusalem they were concentrated in
large numbers. The number six thousand was a
meagre in relation to the vast population of that
country. Therefore, their speciality was lost and
they merged with other people. For this reason
the pure form of *Yajnopavita* could not prevail
any longer. But if the custom of wearing
Yajnopavita was not prevalent in the beginning
of Christian Era, it is impossible to explain why
Christ is depicted in his portraits with a
phylacteries or *Yajnopavita*. Therefore it is
inevitable to accept that *Yajnopavita* was a
common practice then among the Jews.
Edersheim (1898) and Farrar (1874) both have
recorded in the Cambridge Bible that 'Many
people say that our Lord held Phylacteries'.

In the Uffizi Gallery of Florence, there are
portraits in which Christ is shown with a
Phylacteries on his left shoulder, with a Dhoti of a
typical south Indian style around his waist and
with a hair of frontal skull tied in a fashion typical
of south Indian Chidambaram Deekshit style,
exhibiting the hair knot above the forehead. Many
pictures of Christ show *Yajnopavita*, but all his
portraits do not show *Yajnopavita*. Why ? Let us try
to find out its reasons for our satisfaction.

11.6. Indian Origin of Abyssinia

In the past, one of the Christian Bishops,
Frumentius (4 A.D.) who was a Greek, had gone to
Abyssinia. He has written that one author named as
'Virgil' (Full name Publius Vergilius Maro 70 B.C.-
19B.C.) has stated in his book that the people in
Abyssinia were Hindus. Another author Schoff (1912)
has written some comments on a book named as

'Periplus of the Erythaen See' (1ˢᵗ and 3ʳᵈ A.D.). In those comments he writes, 'In Abyssinia, the Christian people used to wear a 'Matab' just like the Hindus of India wear '*Yajnopavita*'. One author Mr. Ferguson who was expert in Engineering and Architecture, says, 'The construction of a Monolith at Axum, capital of Abyssinia, reminds us of the temples of India.' Had there been no relation between India and Abyssinia, Frumentius would not have gone from India to Abyssinia for preaching his religion. Similarly the two authors Ferguson and Schoff would not have got attracted towards the similarities between the two countries, India and Abyssinia. Some Greek authors have stated that one of the queens born in the royal dynasty of Abyssinia was named as 'Kadakaya'. This name is close to a Tamil name 'Kandaki or Kandakka'. There are many such names which force us see the resemblance and conclude that Abyssinia must have been inhabited by the Indians in the past. This is not only a play of ideas. Anyone who reads the book '*Tanya's Appoloneus*' authored by Philastratus admits that evidently Abyssinia was an Indian colony in the past. Abyssinian letters are surprisingly similar to Sanskrit letters. Not only that, but many words are common to Sanskrit and Abyssinian languages. Only a cursory examination will prove it.

12

Indians in Europe and Africa

There are some other independent facts to prove that Arabia and countries around it were colonised by the Indians. Let us examine those facts here. The purpose behind this is to prove the Indian element in the residents there and to find the possibilities of the revival of Krishna element in the name of Keshva Krishna or say Jesus Christ in Palestine and around. Usually when new colonies came up, the migrants give the names to the new cities, mountains, rivers and various other places following their original birthplace. If due to some reason in the new colonies some physical hazards or some religious revolution takes place, those places are destroyed with their names. Such names stay longer in the original place than in the new colonies. The remnants found in an excavation in Mesopotamia reveal a biblical story of a flood, which appears to be a copy of the story present in the old Babylonian culture. In the same way, it will be difficult for many people to see the relation between India and Babylon. 'Babylon' has arisen from 'Babyli'; which has come from 'Papuli', which has further been derived from 'Tiru Papuliur'. Tirupapuliur is a city in south India. 'Tiru' means 'Sri'. It is an honorific prefix. If it is removed, the remaining expression is Papuliur. Ur means city. So the name is 'Papuli'. This got transmuted into Babuli and then to Babylon. In Babylon there is a story of a deluge or flood. This may be a reflection of the original story of the flood which played havoc in India at the time of the end of *Mahaabhaarata* war or the beginning of Kaliyuga (5106 years before or 3044 BCE). The famous Noah's arch was prepared in the city of Suripak which was located on the banks of the river Euphrates. The name or its remnants have now totally disappeared from that country; but are still present in India because many places bearing that name exist in south India. Suripak, Babylon etc. are the names that remind the ancient culture of Mesopotamia, but original places still exist in south India near Chennai. The examples are Surikolam (Vellore's name), Kilpak, Acharpak, Bolini, Tirupapuliur etc.

Another important point to note is that when some people migrate to other place to settle themselves there, they always carry with them the original names of importance, names of holy places, customs and traditions, language, and culture. Naturally the south Indians when migrated to settle in Palestine, must have taken these names with them. If it was so, we must find evidence for it. There is evidence in the Bible that the group system of Tamils, which they carried along with them to Palestine, was prevalent remarkably among the Jews.

As a passing remark, it can be stated here one more fact about the Pandions in Greece. Who were those Pandions? Even Shakespeare has described these Pandions in his poetry, though the later poets forgot them. In the ancient maps Pandions and Kalabraj were included; but the later maps excluded them. The Indian kings and Sages were spreading Indian culture outside India for extending their empires. According to G.D. Savarkar (2003), this fact has been deliberately deleted from the current history books. The kings of Athens namely Pandion the First and Pandion the Second were the Indian kings. The Pandions and Pandionide were south Indian kings, from Pandya dynasty, who had established their kingdoms in Greece. Similarly the Galabri of Greece was from south India, known in the past as Calabra. When the historians will realise this fact, then only they can solve the riddle of these two names and establish the truth. Herodotus has reported that Termilae - Dramuila - Tamila were the ancient residents of Lycca. In connection with them he states about the Carians. These Carians were 'Karayan', which is the name of a race from south India, who were fishermen. If we carry forward our research along these lines, we can solve many riddles of history.

Lycca or Lakka is a corrupt form of 'Lanka'. In the western part of the Asia Minor, some writings are found carved on stones. Those writings reveal that the residents of that region hailed originally from Lakka. Lakka means Lanka. 'N' has disappeared from the name 'Lanka' which became lakka just like Konkan became Kokka, Kuntalam became Kottalam, Kanhadesha (Khandesh) became Kadesh. These are the corrupt forms of the names. Similarly, Lakka is a corrupt form derived from Lanka and Termilae is derived from Tamilae. Thus actually Tamils from Lanka came to stay in Asia Minor, but it is stated in carvings that Termilae came from Lakka. We have already examined other evidences showing that Tamils had gone to the west for settlements. It is supported by this internal evidence.

The famous Ravana, the king of Lanka was a Paulastya. It means that he was born to sage Pulist's dynasty. These Paulastya descendants from south India who migrated to the Asia Minor, are recorded in the stone writings as 'Pulasati'. This name 'Pulasati' later on got converted to 'Philistine' in the Bible. Some researchers agree that

Philistines were Poulastya. This fact definitely proves that the first settlers in the West Asia were Indians.

12.1. Some Evidences for Indian Migrations

Sri Romesh Chandra Dutta, C.I.E. gave a lecture in 1907, in Bangalore on a topic *'Decline of Bauddha religion in India'*. Sri Dutta was a master scholar of ancient history. He told, 'Soon after Buddha established his religion, it spread like fire all over India and king Ashoka accepted it. Ashoka sent many scholars towards the east, the west and the north of India to spread that religion. To the west they went to Palestine, Egypt, Pyrus, Greece, and even beyond it. They were really prone to sacrifice anything. They had no greed, no desire. They were inspired to spread their religion. They had pure knowledge and good aim. Due to combination of all these virtues they could spread their religion easily--------'.

A famous and one of the greatest Jewish historians, Philo writes in his book on history, 'in the hermitages here in Palestine many people of various religions and faiths lived together among whom there were many Braahmanas devotees of Sri Krishna'. Another famous writer states, 'in this way the Brahmanas who went to foreign countries stayed there only permanently. At a later stage, their descendents came back for some reason. But in the mean time in India, the people who used to cross the boundaries of India and visit the foreign countries were considered as out-caste. As such the descendants of the migrated Braahmanas who had returned to India were not accepted by the Braahmanas staying here in India. Therefore they had to perform fire test before acceptance into the Braahmana race. Such Braahmanas are known as *'Nityaacala'* Braahmanas.' Similar facts hold good in connection with the Kshatriyas. Kshatriyas had also undergone such a fire test for their re-admission in Indian society. Such Kshatriyas are still known as Rajputs of Agni-kula or fire-cult. Any way it is established fact that many Braahmanas and   Kshatriyas in the past were going abroad for preaching religion and colonise unmanned lands.

13

Indian Origin of European Portraits
(Depicting Jesus and Mother Mary)

For attainment of God, everything is renounced by gents who are called as *Samnyaasin* or a person who has completely surrendered himself to God. *Samnyaasins* are known all over the world, so I need not write more on it. But *Daasa* or a slave of the God is a concept not known well, so I would like to write elaborately citing examples on the concept of *Daasa*. *Daasa* is a slave of the God who has surrendered the whole of his life to the God. In Sanskrit, '*Daasa*' means a man who realises the Omnipresent God. The meaning of '*Samnyaasin*' is almost the same. So both the words are common to Sanskrit. In Maharashtra, India, Ramadasa is famous. That *Samnyaasin* called himself as a slave, a *Daasa* of Rama. In the same sense those ladies who devoted the whole of their life for the God or for attaining the God were called as *Samnyaasinee* or *Daasee* and were held respectably as 'Mother of society'. This custom was carried by western Vaishnavites of Krishna cult (known as Christians) from their homeland India. That is why, Krishna or Christ was portrayed by them as *Samnyaasin*.

[1]   In Pinakothek at Munich, Jesus Christ is painted in a saffron coloured attire. (Savarkar,

2003; Ramaswami, 1926)

Fig. 13 : Dieric Bouts the Elder, Ecce Agnus Dei, Alte
Pinakothek, Munich, 1462-64

[2] Krishna had a dark complexion, so was
     depicted Christ and so also his mother. In
     Santa Maria Maggots church at Florence,
     there is a portrait where mother Mary is
     painted dark in complexion. (Savarkar, 2003;
     Ramaswami, 1926)

[3] Because the apostles were Tamil in origin and
     their language was Tamil or Aramaic, they
     depicted Krishna in Tamil styled dress.
     (Savarkar, 2003; Ramaswami, 1926)

[4] In the Oratory of San Vincenzo near the
     Lateran Baptistery in Rome, there is a portrait
     of Mary, painted in the 6th century AD, in

Mosaica where Mary is shown in a *Sari*, with a free part of it [*Parda* or *Pallu*] having three stripes. The style of *Sari* is similar to Indian ladies. In this picture there is a sacred ash-mark [*Bhasma Chihna*] on her forehead and neck.

5]   In the 12th century AD one Benedetto Antelami, an Italian architect and sculptor of the Romanesque school, has portrayed Mary in Parma, having a Sari on her body and some ornaments of the Indian style round her neck.

7]   A portrait of about the same period, in a palace of Archiepiscopal at Ravenna, a city diagonally opposite to Rome in Italy named after Ravana, shows a mark called as 'Namam' on her forehead within which there is shown a 'Tilak'. This mark is similar to a typical   mark of Sandal wood paste peculiar to the Vaishnavas of India. Anybody will recognise it immediately, as a typical Vaishnava mark.

Fig. 13: Christ Pantocrator, ca. 1100, from the dome of a church at Daphni, near Athens, Christ is depicted with a Tilak. a U-shape, between the eyebrows, often square-bottomed.

8]   In a Podesty Art Gallery at Ankona, there are portraits painted by Carlo Crivelli, in which

Mary is shown with a rosary round her neck similar to that used by scholars in Madras or devotees [Pandaram] who wore a chain of *Rudraaksha* for chanting a name of the God. Jesus the Christ is said to be 'Ben-Pandera' in old Christian literature. In Tamil 'Ben' means son and 'Pandera' means devotee or worshipper. Considering these portraits is it not proved that Christ was called as Ben-Pandera appropriately, precisely, meaningfully ?

9]   In India, males sit in a cross legged position while females sit in a peculiar pose. They keep their left thigh touching the ground, with knees flexed, so that left leg comes in approximation with left thigh. They keep their right thigh erect in a vertical posture with knee flexed so that right leg also is upright, vertical in contact with right thigh. The right foot is kept with sole touching the ground near the horizontal left foot. See fig. 14 below:

Fig. 14

This posture is appreciated as a polite, respectable, and gentle particularly among south Indian women. In Florence, there is a portrait sketched by Taddeo Gaddi in which Mary is shown in Santa Croce in Florence waiting for the auspicious time for her marriage ceremony. In this picture she is painted in a south Indian female sitting style as is described above. Please note that modern European or Muslim ladies do not sit in such a typical posture.

10] In Florence, there is a picture painted by Fra Angelico known in Italy as il Beato Angelico in which crucifixion of Jesus is displayed in a heart rending manner. In it, Mary is shown with a face sunken due to pathetic mood; but her style of sitting is the same as described above, a typical south Indian female style.

In Tamils the name 'Mariamma' was and is still in use. As apostles were Tamil speaking, they named Christ's mother as Mariamma. That name got changed to Marium and then to Mary in the European style. In the European literature her name is recorded as Marium. We have considered the portraits of Mary above. If her pictures are available in plenty, it is quite natural that portraits of Jesus will be found in more abundance.

Let us now consider the portraits of Jesus, how and where they are depicted.

Among the immigrants in the west there were Shaivites too. Shaivites depicted Jesus as the incarnation of Shiva and painted in his pictures Nandi, the sacred bull, peacock, etc. Vaishnavites, however, depicted Christ as the incarnation of Vishnu and therefore his pictures in the form of Vishnu are more prevalent. Christ is also shown as a Fish (*Matsyaavataara*), having an eagle as his vehicle (*Garuda Vaahana*), Lion-faced like *Narasimha*, with a conch in hand (*Shankhadhara*), in a sleeping posture when a lotus came out from his umbilicus, navel. He is shown in a dwarf form like '*Vaoou Vaamana*'. He is shown wearing a cap in which a peacock's feather is planted just like that of his original character of Lord Krishna. Pictures of cow and donkey are also sketched nearby. He is shown as crushing the head of a serpent just like Krishna in '*Kaaliaa-Mardana*'. Jesus is also shown in an enormous shape as is told in the *Geeta*, the famous '*Vishvaroopa-Darshana*'. Jesus is also depicted in the form of Lord Dattaatreya, the three headed God of the Hindus. Thus there are so many pictures in *Avataara*-form, like that of Krishna or Vishnu.

1] It is well known that Mary became pregnant without being married. Christians believe that Mary had an intercourse with an angel and became pregnant to deliver Jesus Christ. Mary had a faith that she was impregnated by a divine personality and that Jesus was a child of that divine person. This will be elaborated ahead.

2] Christians do believe that Mary wedded a divine man. This story is similar to that of a chaste woman 'Andal' in Tamil who believed that she married the God in her dream.

3] It is believed in Roman Catholics that to win favour of Jesus, one must first get favour of Mary. This again is a Hindu concept. Goddess Lakshmi is worshipped to get riches and wealth among the Hindus in the same manner Christians began worship of Mary with the same purpose. Lakshmi is supposed to be the wife of Lord Vishnu, similarly Mary was supposed to be the wife of the God. After deification of Mary some of her pictures are painted with a plantain fruit in her hand and a monkey near her. It is not palatable for the Christians. But they do not understand its pith or essence and therefore they hate this picture. Usually before Lord Rama there is an Ape-God Hanuman as well as an Eagle. Christians do not realise that Mary is supposed to be a Goddess and so there is an ape before her for offering all service to her.

13.1. Indian Origin of Attires associated with Jesus and his Family Members

According to the legend propagated by the Apostles of Christ, physical marriage of Marry took place with a man named as Joseph. Joseph was said to be a Jew and the Jews were originally Tamil Indians. So, we can get a root of the name 'Joseph' in Tamil. It is well known that European languages register many Indian words in a corrupt form. G.D. Savarkar (2003) gave some examples for those who do not know this fact. A name Mathura of an Indian city is converted in English to 'Mutra', Mumbai is distorted to Bombay, Mukhopaadhyaaya, Bandopaadhyaaya and Chatopaadhyaaya become respectively as Mukherjee, Banerjee and Chaterjee. Ordinarily, the in conversant people will find it impossible to accept that one word has originated from another. Hence we will have to see the root of the name 'Joseph' carefully. Pronunciation 'a' (Je) took the form of 'o' (Jo). In the same manner, 'o' may take the form of 'a'. Naturally, Joseph may be derived from Sheshep and Sheshcp from Sheshappa. Thus Sheshappa appears to have taken the form of Joseph. Since this legendary figure Joseph came out of western Indian immigrants, his pictures are also found in Indian attire. The tradition also depicts Jesus in the real Indian form. In the Indian tradition, a bridegroom always wears yellow coloured clothes with turmeric. In the same fashion Joseph is shown in yellow attire in a portrait sketched by a religious European artist. Jesus was said to have a sister and her name was 'Tamar'. Thamar or Thamarai is a Tamil word meaning a lotus. It proves that the sister of Jesus was named as 'Kamala' in the Hindu tradition. In India usually girls are named like Kamala, Padma, etc. The European names of girls are not given after lotus.

Tamilian immigrants of India in the west pictured Christ like a Tamil Hindu, so his hair were tied in a knot like typical Tamil fashion, as already pointed out. Sir Wyke Bayliss (21 October 1835-5 April 1906), British painter, has painted a portrait of Christ in which his hair are shown tied like Tamils with a tuft of hair let loose on his back. This portrait is present in the Revas Regnam burial ground of Rome. Just like the hair style there is a typical style of dress of Tamil people. That typical style of Dhoti is shown in pictures of Jesus painted by Bernardino Luini (c. 1480/82-1532), a North Italian painter, Diego Rodríguez de Silva y Velázquez (June 6, 1599-August 6, 1660), a Spanish painter, and others.

14

The Bible of Krisht/Christ

It is seen until now, that the Christ marks the revival of Krishna and Christianity, the Krishna cult in the west. Under the circumstances, the Paulinism in the Bible or the various versions of the Bible cannot be the Bible of Krishna. They represent the concerned Individuals' knowledge about Indian philosophy and morality. Whatever they produced in the name of Bible of Christ was the outcome of the knowledge obtained by them from various Indian sources. For example, Ancient Indian teachings have been borrowed by the Apostles through Buddhism, so as to assign them to Jesus. Edmunds has discussed Buddhist element in Christianity in detail. Some of his findings as also quoted by Holger (1994) can be illustrated here too. But here it may be pointed out that so-called Buddhist element is nothing but the Indian element in Bible.

For instance, Buddha's sending out of his disciple was imitated/borrowed by the writer of Mark's Bible (6: 7-13) while sending out legendary Jesus' disciples. The remarkable parallel between the two runs as under :

Buddha says:

"Go O monks, and travel afar, for the benefit and welfare of many, out of compassion for the world, to be the advantage and welfare of gods and of mortals. And let not two of you take the same path. Preach the teachings that leads to good

......Preach it in spirit and letter. Show in your perfect sinlessness how the religious life should be lived".

The monks lived as beggars, totally reliant on alms of the ordinary people. They owed nothing more than the clothes on their backs. Their life was one of the renunciation, but there was no need for ascetic austerity.

The Bible (6:7-13) of Mark quotes :

And he called unto him the twelve, and began to send them forth by two and two, and gave them power over unclean spirits;

And commanded them that they should take nothing for their journey, save a staff only; no scrip, no bread, no money in their purse:

But be shod with sandals, and not put on two coats.

And he said unto them, In what place so ever ye enter into an house there abide till ye depart from that place.

And whosoever shall not receive you, nor hear you, when ye depart thence, shake off the dust under your feet for a testimony against them. (Holger, 1994:72-73).

Buddhists rule required that followers joined the community by 'going out into open' - by quitting their houses and families (and with them the trappings of lay life) to enter the brotherhood of monks wandering without permanent shelter, to be free of all earthly concerns, to meditate on the teachings, and gradually to free themselves from the mortal passions and worldly desires.

Bible of Matthew (19:24) says," It is easier for a camel to go through the eye of needle, than for a rich man to enter into the kingdom of God". Buddhism has borrowed this feature from *Upanishads*. Accordingly, 'The mouth of truth is covered with the vessel of gold. If one wants to see the reality (God) he has to remove this golden cover'.

hiranyamayena   paatrena   satyasyaabhihitam mukham
tattvam   pushannapaavrinu   satyadharmaaya drishtaye.

In *Lalitavistara*, Buddha says :

" *The knowledge of the truth, the attainment of Nirvaana - this is the supreme blessing. Through love alone can hate be vanquished; through perfect love evil may be overcome .. .. Speak no harsh words to your neighbour, and he will respond to you in like terms".*

Not only the above one, a merchant from Sunapaortha asked Buddha to teach him. 'People are violent', said the *Dvija*. 'If they offended you, how would you respond?'

The merchant shrugged his shoulders. 'I would make no reply at all to them', he said.

'And if they hit you?'

'I would not react then either'.

'And if they kill you?'

The merchant smiled, 'Death, master, is no evil. Some even desire it'.

Matthew's Gospel on the lines of Buddhism teaches, 'Love your neighbour as you yourself ; if anyone strikes your one cheek, turn the other towards him too'. This feature was borrowed by Buddhism from Vedic dharma. It says, '*atmavatsarvabhooteshu yah pashyati sah pashyati*'. 'Let us see all living beings as we ourselves'.

Buddha like that of Krishna says to his favourite disciple Ananda, 'Believe in me Ananda. All those who believe me will come to great joy'. Bible also instruct its followers to believe in Christ and not to waver in this faith.

At another occasion, the Buddha described the giving of alms as 'a seed sown on good ground, which brings forth fruit in plenty'. He also declared that 'Food that is eaten does not destroy a person..... but the taking of life, stealing, lying, adultery, and even thinking of doing these things, can certainly lead to a person's destruction.' And 'A man buries a treasure in a deep pit. But a treasure hidden away like this can be no use to him. Now a treasure of love for one's neighbour, of piety and of moderation - that is a treasure that no thief can ever steal'. And 'Even when the heavens crash to the earth, even when the world is swallowed up and destroyed, even then, Ananda, the words of the Buddha remain true'.

All these sayings of Buddha are assigned to Krishna or Christ of the Gospels. It seems that the propagators of Christianity were familiar with *Lalitavistara*. (Holger, 1994: 96).

As per *Lalitavistara*, Buddha was subjected to temptation by Mara, the Lord of sensory pleasure. Mara offered delicious dishes to Siddhartha in the middle of his fasting and meditation and showed him the riches and distractions of this world, but the contemplative concentration was not in the least disturbed. The same test and the same result has been assigned to Jesus in the desert.

Buddha nominated his first 5 noble disciples and gave them command 'Come, follow me'. The disciples renounced everything on the spot and followed him. Same theme was borrowed from Buddha and applied to Jesus by his propagators.   Peter, Andrew and sons of Zebedee were to follow Jesus so long afterwards.

Buddha spoke in parables. Once he says, 'When blinds hold on to each other in a line, the one at the front sees nothing, the one in the middle sees nothing, and the one at the end sees nothing.' Like Buddha, Jesus is also shown speaking in parables. He once described how a blind man cannot lead another blind without both falling into a ditch.

Just as the birth of Buddha was prophesied by the old Asit, who shortly before his death comes to the newly born child, takes him in his arms, and declares :

This is the peerless one, pre-eminent among men .. .. He will attain to the ultimate height of enlightenment. He has knowledge of the supreme Will. It is he who will set the wheel of Dharma in motion. He would have compassion on the struggle of humankind. The faith he founds will spread all over the world.

The same uttering have been borrowed from Buddhism and assigned to Christ through the mouth of Simeon. He also takes the child in his arms and declares thus :

Lord now lettest thou thy servant departs in peace, according to thy word:

For mine eyes have seen thy salvation,

Which thou hast prepared before the face of all people.

A light to lighten the Gentiles, and glory of thy people Israel (Luke 2:29-32)

This speech is an apparent borrowing from Buddhism.

We find that at school, the young Siddhartha was already familiar with all kinds of religious texts. He went off on a short excursion of his own, was missed and then found deep in meditation. The same story was borrowed and ascribed to the Jesus. He is also found in learned debate with scriptural experts in the temple while his parents have been looking for him.

Buddha began teaching publicly at about the age of thirty, the same age has been assigned in case of Jesus. Like Buddha, Jesus has been shown travelling the country together with his principal disciples in voluntary poverty, instructing them meanwhile by using vivid imagery and parables. Like Buddha, Jesus is shown with twelve principle disciples, and his first followers are two brothers - again in an exact parallel with Buddha's first followers.

Buddha preached his disciples sitting under a fig tree and he himself got the enlightenment under a Pipal tree (another species of fig tree). On the same pattern, Jesus has also been shown enlightening his disciple Nathanael sitting under a fig tree. Buddha has a one favourite disciples and he was betrayed by another disciple. The same story has been associated with Jesus. He is also shown to a have a one favourite disciple and another disciple betrays him.

Buddha was against the blood sacrifice performed by some Braahmanas during his period. On the same pattern Jesus is shown to have denounced blood sacrifice of the Jews.

Buddha's observation of Braahmanas was, "Inside they are like rough wood, though their outer appearance is smooth'. On the same pattern Jesus is shown exposing the hypocrisy of the Pharisees. At one place he says, 'You are like unto whited sepultures, which indeed appear beautiful outward, but are within full of dead men's bones, and of all uncleanness'. (Matthew: 23:27)

Buddha criticised the ritualism of orthodox Braahmanas. On the same pattern, Jesus has been shown criticising the Pharisees (orthodox Jews).

These are few of the examples of borrowing from Indian sources cited here. According to Edmunds (1908), there can be around 112 passages cited in the New Testament that exhibit evidences of their borrowings from Buddhists sources. Here one should not forget that Buddhist philosophy is not different from Hindu philosophy except the ritual aspect.

Thus the present Bible assigned to Christ is a compilation of references borrowed from Indian sources depending upon the knowledge of compilers. They were a confused lot unlike their predecessors: John and Paul. With John's intervention of posing himself as Christ, the later followers of Christ forgot the real Character of Krishna of *Mahaabhaarata* whom they were introducing and propagating as Jesus. The present Bible is the admixture of tenets from many Indian sources. If the followers of Krishna cult (Christianity) in the west want to discover the actual Bible of Christ. They must read Upanishads and Geeta.

Bibliography

Acharya S, "*The origins of Christianity and the quest for the historical Jesus Christ,*" at: http://www.artnet.net/~acharya/truth/origins.htm

Arya, Ravi Prakash (2005a). "*India The Civiliser of the World*", International Vedic Vision New York & Indian Foundation for Vedic Science, Delhi.

.... (2005b). "*Revisiting the Roots of Judeo-Christianity*", International Vedic Vision New York & Indian Foundation for Vedic Science, Delhi.

.... (2009). "*Origin of Indo Europeans*", International Vedic Vision New York & Indian Foundation for Vedic Science, Delhi.

Amhein, Michael (1984). "*Is Christianity True?*" London.

Apostle James, "*First Apostle to the Antichrist - The Jesus Myth,*" at: http://www.antichrist.com/myth.htm

Barret David B. (1982). "*World Christian Encyclopaedia: A Comparative Study of Churches and Religions in the World, 1900-2000*", OUP.

"*Barlaam and Josaphat* "(1913). Catholic Encyclopaedia. New

York: Robert Appleton Company.

Bible Alive, "Did Jesus Exist?" at: http://www.biblealive.org.nz/pages/e50121.html

Bible Review (1997). Vol. XIII, Number 3, p. 43

Blavatsky, H P (1877). "*Isis Unveiled*", J.W. Bouton.

------------------ (1880). "*From the Caves and Jungles of Hindostan*", Floating Press.

------------------(1933) [1889]. "*The Voice of the Silence*",

Theosophy Co. (India) Ltd.

------------------(1889). *"The Key to Theosophy"*, Theosophical Pub. Co,

Briant, Pierre (1996). "*Alexander the Great : Man of Action, man of Spirit*" Harry N. Abrams.

Brugsch bey, Heinrich (1875). **"Histoire d'Égypte", Leipzig.**

Cathy, *"Did Jesus really exist?,"* http://www.geocities.com/Heartland/Prairie/6201/exist.html

Chaman Lal (1940). *"Hindu America",* New Book Co. Bombay.

Copeland, M.A. "*Christian Apologetics: The Historical Jesus,*"http://ccel.wheaton.edu/contrib/exec_outlines/ca/ca_02.htm

Cory, I.P. (1876). "*Ancient Fragments*", Reeves & Turner, London.

Deissman, A (1925)."*Paulus*", Tubingen, 2nd Edition.

Doherty, Earl "*The Jesus Puzzle: Was there no historical Jesus?*" Journal of Higher Criticism at: http://pages.ca.inter.net/~oblio/jesus.html

Doherty, Earl (1999). "*The Jesus Pizzle*" Canadian Humanist Publications.

Edersheim, Alfred (1898). "*Jesus the Messiah*", London.

Edmunds, Albert J. (1908). "*Buddhists and Christian Gospels",* Philadelphia, Innes & sons; [etc.,etc.]

Elst, Keoenraad (1993). "*Psychology of Prophetism: A Secular Look at the Bible*", New Delhi.

Eusebius . Lemp Berk's Edition quoted by Harbilas Sarda (2007).

Eyre, R.A. "*Did Jesus Christ exist?*" at: http://www.cs.york.ac.uk/~gem/rob/jc/jcexist/submenu.html

Farrar, F.W. (1874). 'The Life of Christ'.

Flavius, Josephus (37 or 38-circa 101 C.E). "*Antiquities of the Jews*".

Gauvin, Marshall J., "*Did Jesus Christ Really Live*" (from: www.infidels.org/)

George Fletcher, *"Did Jesus Christ exist?,"* at: http://pages.prodigy.com/myotherapy/jesus.htm

Goel, Sita Ram   (2001). *"Jesus Christ : An Artifice for Aggression"*, Voice of India, New Delhi, Reprint.

Gould, Stephen Jay (1995). *"Dinosaur in a Haystack"* (Chapter 2), Harmony Books, New York.

Graham, Henry Grey, Rev.(1960). *"Where we got the Bible,"* B. Heder Book Company.

Graves, Kersey   (1875).   *"The World's Sixteen Cricified Saviors"*.

Goswami, Bhakti Anand (2000). " Radha-Krisna / Rhoda-Kouros.. Hari / Heri / Heli / Eli / and Atenism Explained, Orlando,.

Guy Fau   (1967).*"Le Fable de Jesus Christ,"* 3rd edition.

Heath Sidney (1907). *"Our Homeland Churches and How to Study Them"*, The Homeland Association.

Heeren A.H.L.(1846).   *"Historical Researches"*,   4th Edition, Henry G. Bohn, London.

Helms, Randel McCraw, *"Who Wrote the Gospels"*, Millennium Press

Historicus, *"Did Jesus ever live or is Christianity funded upon a myth?,"* United Secularists of America at: http://www.freethinkers.org/library/historical/historicus/jesus.html

Holger Kersten   (1994). *"Jesus Lived India"*, Element.

Holger Kersten & Elmar R. Gruber (1994). *"The Jesus Conspiracy"*, Element.

Irenaeus of Lyon (140?-202? C.E.), *"Against Heresies"*.

Jacolliot, Louis   (1876). *"La Bible Dans L'Inde"*, Librairie Internationale, Paris.

John Allegro (1970). *"The Sacred Mushroom and the Cross"*.

Jones, William   (1788). "Asiatic Researches", Vol.1

------------------   (1790). "Asiatic Researches", Vol.2

------------------   (1795). "Asiatic Researches", Vol.3

------------------   (1797). "Asiatic Researches", Vol.4

Johnson, Paul   (1978). *"A History of Christianity"*,

Penguin Book, London.

Julius von Klaproth (1823). *Asia polyglotta*, A. Schubart.

Leedom, Tim C. (1993). *"The Book Your Church Doesn't Want You To Read"* Kendall/Hunt Publishing Company.

Levi, *"The Acquarian Gospel of Jesus The Christ"*, London, L.N. Fowler & Co. Ltd. 7th edition.

Mackey, James P. (1979). *Jesus the Man and Myth*, London.

Massey, Gerald (1900). *"Geral Massey's Lectures : The Historical Jesus and Mythical Christ"*.

McDowell, J. & Stewart, D. *"Did Jesus really exist?,"* from "Answers to Tough Questions, at: http://members.aol.com/jcsaves7/didJesusreallyexist.htm

McKinsey, C. Dennis (1995). *"The Encyclopaedia of Biblical Errancy"* Prometheus Books.

Metzger, Bruce (1968). *"The Text of New Testament - Its Transmission, Corruption and Restoration"* Oxford University Press.

Michael Martin (1991). *"The case against Christianity,"* Temple.

Meille, G.E. (1924). *"Christ's Likeness in History and Art"*, Burns, Oates & Washbourne, London.

Nestle, W. 1947 : *"Krisis des Christentums"*, p.89.

Notovich, N (1895). "The Unknown life of Jesus Christ" London.

Oak, P.N. (1978). *"Christianity is Chrisn-nity"*, New Delhi.

--------------(2003). *"World Vedic Heritage"*, Hindi Sahitya Sadan, New Delhi.

Olcott, Col. (1881). *"Theosophist"*, a Journal published by Theosophical Society of India, March, 1881.

Pagels, Elaine (1888). *"Adam, Eve, and the Serpent"* Vintage Books, New York.

------------------(1979). *"The Gnostic Gospels"*,intage Books, New York.

------------------(1975). *"The Origin of Satan"*, Random House, New York.

Parmar, Nagina Ram (2004)."¶*ryavarata kaa praaceena itihaasa"* edited by Ravi Prakash Arya, Baba Saheb Apte Smarak Samiti, Delhi.

"Periplus of the Erythaen See" (1ˢᵗ -3ʳᵈ A.D.)

Philostratus (1921). *"Lives of the Sophists. Eunapius, Lives of the Philosophers and Sophists".* translated by Wilmer C. Wright. Loeb Classical Library

------------   ---(1912).   *"Appollonius   of   Tyana"*, translated by Translated by Christopher P. Jones. 2005-6, Loeb Classical Library.

Pococke, E (2004). *"Indian Origin of Greece and Ancient World"* Ed. by Dr. Ravi Prakash Arya, Indian Foundation for Vedic Science.

Prajnananda Swami, *Christ the Saviour and Christ Myth.*

Price, R.M. 1997 : *"Christ a Fiction,"* at: http://www.infidels.org/library/modern/robert_pric e/fiction.html

Price, Robert M.(2000). *"Deconstructing Jesus"* Prometheus Books.

Pritchard, John Paul (1972). *"A Literary Approach to the New Testament,"* Norman, University of Oklahoma Press.

Prosper Alfaric (1959). *"Origines Social du Christianisme".*

Rae West, *"Existence of Jesus Controversy,"* "http://www.homeusers.prestel.co.uk/littleton/gm1 _jesu.htm

Ramaswamy Iyer, M.S. (1926). *"Was Jesus a Vishvakarma Braahmana?"* 'Theosophist Magazine,' ed. Annie Wood Besant, July 1926 to September 1926, pp.724-725.

Remsberg, John E., *"The Christ"* Prometheus Books

Robertson, J.M. (1902)." *A Short History of Christianity"* Watts & Co.

--------------------(1903). *"Pagan Christs,"* London.

--------------------(1910). *"Christianity and Mythology,"* 2nd edition, *"Testament: The Bible and History,"* videotape
http://info.wlu.ca/~wwwav/WLUCollection/G/v346

.htm

-----------------------(1966). "*Pagan Christs*", New York.

Robinson, B.A "*DID JESUS OF NAZARETH ACTUALLY EXIST? All sides to the question*" religious tolerance.org

Romer, John (1988). "*Testament : The Bible and History*" Henry Holt and Company, New York,.

Russell, Bertrand (1927). "Why I am not a Christian?" London: Watts & Co. This was a Lecture delivered by Russell on March 6, 1927 to the National Secular Society, South London Branch, at Battersea Town Hall. Published in pamphlet form in that same year, the essay subsequently achieved new fame with Paul Edwards' edition of Russell's book, Why I Am Not a Christian and Other Essays ... (1957).

Sarda, Harbilas (2007). " *Hindu Superiority*", International Vedic Vision New York & Indian Foundation for Vedic Science, Delhi.

Savarkar, G.D. (2003). " *Jesus the Christ was a Hindu*" IFFVS, Rohtak, Delhi.

Schweitzer, Albert (1945). "*The Quest for Historical Jesus,* London.

Schonfield, Hugh Joseph (1963). "*A Passover plot,*" London.

Shaikh Anwar, "*The Vedic Civilization*".

Smith Philip (1879). " *The student's ancient history: The ancient history of the East. From the earliest times to the conquest by Alexander the Great. Including Egypt, Assyria, ... Media, Persia, Asia Minor, and Phoenicia*", Harper.

Smith, W.B. (1957)."*The Birth of the Gospels*".

Spong, Bishop Shelby (1991). "*Rescuing the Bible from Fundamentalism*" Harper San Francisco.

Suetonius (1998). "*The Lives of the Caesars,* Harvard University Press, Revised edition.

Tacitus (55?-117? C.E.),"*Annals*"

Taylor, Joan (1993). "*Christians and Holy Places*", OUP.

Todd (Col.), James (1829). "*Annals and Antiquities of Rajasthan*".

Walker, B.G. (1983). "*The Woman's Encyclopaedia of*

Myths and Secrets," Harper & Row, Page 663-664.

Wells, G.A (1982). "*The Historical Evidence for Jesus,*" Prometheus.

Wells, G.A. (1985). "*Historicity of Jesus*" in "*Encyclopaedia of Unbelief,*" Prometheus.

Wells, G.A. (1986)."*Did Jesus Exist?*" London.

Wilson, Dorothy Frances (1938). "*The Gospel Sources, some results of modern scholarship,*" London, Student Christian Movement press.

"*The Revel Bible Dictionary*" (1990). Wynnewood Press, New York.

"*King James Bible*" (1611).

"*U.S. News & World Report*" (1990).

"*Various issues of Bible Review magazine*", published by the Biblical Archaeology Society, Washington D.C.

Hindu, the Madras Daily. July 30 to Aug. 5, 1940.

Vedic Science. A quarterly Journal of Indian Foundation for Vedic Science, published by International Vedic Vision, New York.

Printed in Great Britain
by Amazon